THE GROWTH OF REGIONAL TRADING BLOCS IN THE GLOBAL ECONOMY

Richard S. Belous
Rebecca S. Hartley

Editors

The Growth of Regional Trading Blocs in the Global Economy

NPA Report #243

Price $15.00

ISBN 0-89068-100-7
Library of Congress
Catalog Card Number 89-64099

A voluntary association incorporated under the laws
of the District of Columbia
1424 16th Street, N.W., Suite 700
Washington, D.C. 20036

Printed in the United States of America

Contents

TABLES

MAP

Sea Changes

We are often told that the tides are inexorably pushing all of us into a global economy. This may be true. But tides are known for their ebbs, flows and undertows.

While economic, political and technological forces have internationalized many markets, these same forces also appear to be expanding the role of regional trading blocs. The multilateral trading system, as embodied in the General Agreement on Tariffs and Trade since the 1940s, is not the only trade strategy currently being considered by governments, corporations and labor unions. Lester Thurow, Dean of MIT's Sloan School of Management, states the basic issue quite clearly:

> If you look around the world at the moment, you see all kinds of places where we are essentially breaking up into trading blocs. . . . Everybody in the world knows that this is happening, but nobody wants to face reality.[1]

Some trade experts insist that the GATT describes "a black and white world of trade: free trade versus protectionism. . . . The Anglo-American system represents a distinct minority of the world's trading systems."[2] These experts argue that the GATT must be "tailored" to incorporate many different systems. Still others have called for a world of "managed trade" based on a system of regional trading blocs.[3]

As explained in detail in Chapter 1, we recently surveyed the members of the National Planning Association's policy committees concerning their expectations in the area of international trade. These executives—many of whom are chairs, vice chairs, presidents, or CEOs of leading U.S. corporations—seem to be facing Thurow's "reality." In fact, the majority of the executives surveyed fear that he is right and that the multilateral system is fragmenting into regional trading blocs.

There is, of course, more than one policy response to these expectations and concerns. One strategy might be to accept as inevitable a fragmentation of the world system into regional blocs and strive to form a system of managed trade between the blocs. A second strategy could be a renewed effort to revitalize the GATT so that it can deal with changing international realities. A third strategy might attempt to maximize the benefits and minimize the costs created by regional trading blocs while maintaining some sort of multilateral trading system. A fourth could be to work to ensure that regional trading blocs are as GATT-consistent as possible, and/or that they cover areas currently unregulated by the GATT. These and other strategies are examined in this study.

There is a common denominator in these policy responses, and that is the need for new international institutions—or a vastly reformed GATT—to establish new international rules of the road.

This study does not present one party line or one point of view. Instead, it offers a diversity of views from many different parts of the economy. Our goal is to encourage private and public sector leaders to assess and plan for the new realities in the vital area of international trade.

However, it is only fair that the reader know our basic point of view. Despite all the problems of the GATT, we believe the world has been much better off due to the GATT's existence than it would have been in a fragmented trading system. We view an equitable, multilateral system as the best choice for the global economy. Yet, we do not believe that this best choice can withstand the impact of various forces. Therefore, in the near future we may face a world of "second-best" solutions in which the role of regional trading blocs will continue to grow. Although the United States has declined in relative strength in recent years compared to many of its trading partners, America remains the leader of the Western coalition that is dedicated to democratic values and enlightened market economies. Thus, America's approach to regional trading blocs continues to be essential to the world trading scene.

Outside the academic community, there are few advocates of pure multilateralism or pure regionalism. We believe that many governments, corporations and unions will follow a two-tiered international trading policy that will mix multilateralism and regional trading blocs. The results could be quite volatile. The trick will be to stay out of the undertow.

Richard S. Belous
Rebecca S. Hartley

NOTES

1. Lester Thurow, in *World Link* (June 1989), p. 9.
2. Pat Chote and Juyne Linger, "Tailored Trade: Dealing with the World as It Is," *Harvard Business Review* (January-February 1988).
3. Robert Kuttner, *Managed Trade and Economic Sovereignty* (Washington, D.C.: Economic Policy Institute, 1989).

Executive Summary

Regional trading blocs appear to be a growing force in the global economy. The new U.S.-Canada Free Trade Agreement, plans to form a unified market in the European Community and a potential Asian yen trading zone are clear signs that the role of regional blocs is increasing. In addition, numerous regional agreements have been formed in Latin America, Africa, South Asia, and Southeast Asia.

This study is one of the first in-depth examinations of this international trend and its impact on corporations, workers and governments. As part of the study, the National Planning Association surveyed the members of its policy committees, many of whom are chairs, vice chairs, presidents, or CEOs of leading American corporations. The majority of these executives—88 percent—believe the world economy is shifting more in the direction of regional trading blocs. Roughly 75 percent think this trend will hurt the General Agreement on Tariffs and Trade, which has provided the international rules of the road for a vast portion of world trade since the late 1940s. Thus, a larger role for regional blocs could have a major impact on the international economy.

MULTILATERALISM VERSUS REGIONALISM

One way to understand regional trading blocs is to compare them with the GATT. As indicated in the following chart, the key principle behind the multilateral GATT system is nondiscrimination, while regional trading blocs are founded on the principle of preferences. Bloc members can practice discrimination in granting different preferences to various nations. The GATT system is open to all nations who are willing to follow certain basic rules, whereas a regional trading bloc may not be open to all who wish to join and agree to follow the bloc's basic rules.

Backers of multilateralism tend to base their views on concepts such as free trade, comparative advantage and economic liberalism. Backers of regional trading blocs—which often take the form of free trade areas, customs unions or sectorial agreements—favor free trade in certain cases but also often endorse what is called neomercantilism. They base their economic world view on concepts such as strategic trade theory, managed trade and economic nationalism rather than the traditional concept of comparative advantage.

As the hegemonic leader of the Western world after World War II, the United States was a major force behind the GATT,

A COMPARISON OF THE PRINCIPLES AND CHARACTERISTICS OF THE GATT AND THE REGIONAL TRADING BLOC MODEL

GATT Principles and Characteristics	Regional Trading Bloc Principles and Characteristics
(1) Trade is based on the principle of nondiscrimination.	(1) Trade is based on the principle of discrimination.
(2) All members are bound to grant as favorable treatment to each other as they give to any other member, i.e., most-favored-nation status.	(2) Nations within the bloc share special preferences not granted to nations outside the bloc.
(3) To the maximum extent possible, protection should be provided only through tariffs.	(3) Protection is often provided through quantitative restrictions as well as tariffs.
(4) Basic ideas include economic liberalism, multilateralism and free trade based on comparative advantage.	(4) Basic ideas include economic nationalism or regionalism, bilateralism, and trade often based on strategic trade theory and neomercantilism.
(5) The system is designed as a community open to all who are willing to follow membership rules.	(5) The bloc may not be open to all who wish to join and are willing to follow membership rules.
(6) The goal is to build a unified and integrated global system.	(6) The bloc may function as an exclusive club that generates a "them versus us" psychology.
(7) Under Article XXIV, the system provides a three-part test to determine if a regional trading bloc is consistent with the GATT.	(7) In the view of some advocates, blocs are a way of building a stronger multilateral system in the long run.

and many American government, business and labor leaders backed the multilateral trading system. However, because of the relatively declining U.S. share of the global economy, American leadership has been unable to push multilateralism with the same force it used prior to 1980, and a growing number of public and private sector leaders are now flirting with the notion of regional trading blocs. Furthermore, many U.S. leaders question the comparatively high cost to the United States under the multilateral trading system in relation to other GATT members, who, they argue, should be paying a larger share.

TWO-TIERED POLICIES

Outside the academic community, there are few advocates of either pure multilateralism or pure regional trading blocs. In most cases, political, business and labor leaders support policies that mix features of both systems. Under such a two-tiered policy, for example, economic liberalism and free trade may increase within a regional trading bloc; conversely, economic nationalism or economic regionalism may become a stronger force outside a bloc.

Implementation of a two-tiered policy could greatly alter the international trading system. If, through a policy mix, the United States makes a significant move away from multilateralism, the GATT will be seriously harmed. The hope is that a two-tiered policy for the United States can be constructed so as not to harm the GATT.

HUMAN RESOURCE IMPACTS

The growth of regional trading blocs also could substantially influence labor markets and labor-management relations. Increased dependence on blocs rather than on the GATT could present management with many new options concerning employment patterns, compensation structures and unionization levels.

In reaction to these new realities, labor is starting to strive for regional labor, health and safety standards. In the European Community, labor is currently playing a major role in the drafting of EC-wide labor market and social policy standards. In the United States, labor has shown a strong interest in trade policy and legislation.

DIVERSE VIEWS

This study presents a number of views on the issue. Chapter 1 is a basic introduction to regional trading blocs written by the editors. It traces the economic and political reasons behind the regional trading bloc trend. Chapter 2, by C. Michael Aho, Director of Economic Studies at the Council on Foreign Relations, presents the case against the growth of regional trading blocs. Chapter 3, by Richard Cooper, Director of Tax Economics, Price Waterhouse, details the points in favor of regional trading blocs. Dr. Cooper explains how to maximize the benefits and minimize the costs of regional trading blocs.

Mark Anderson, head of the Office of International Trade at the AFL-CIO, offers a view from labor in Chapter 4. He highlights the problems the GATT has created for American workers in recent years. In Chapter 5, Richard Belous, NPA Vice President of

International Affairs, explains how regional trading blocs may act as a new "wild card" in labor-management relations.

In Chapter 6, Herbert Weiner, a Consultant on labor matters to the Department of State and a former career Foreign Service Officer, discusses the philosophy underlying the United States' support of the Marshall Plan and of Europe's efforts to build a unified community. In Chapter 7, Michael Calingaert examines how EC 1992 could affect the European Community's trade policy and actions. Mr. Calingaert is the Director of European Operations for the Pharmaceutical Manufacturers Association and a former NPA Visiting Senior Fellow.

Maureen Farrow, former President of the C.D. Howe Institute and a Senior Economist with Coopers and Lybrand, and Robert York, a Policy Analyst at the C.D. Howe Institute and Canadian Research Director of the Canadian-American Committee, analyze the policy implications of the U.S.-Canada FTA and EC 1992 for Canada and the United States in Chapter 8.

Dick Nanto, a Senior Economist with the Congressional Research Service of the Library of Congress, focuses on the reactions of Japan and its neighbors to the growth of regional trading blocs in Chapter 9. Richard Tropp, the Chief Executive Officer of Washington Development Capital Corporation, takes a close look at U.S. government and business approaches to regional trading agreements in Latin America, Africa, South Asia, and Southeast Asia in Chapter 10. Rebecca Hartley, an NPA Fellow in the international program, examines in Chapter 11 the evolution of the Eastern European trading bloc, the Council for Mutual Economic Assistance. In Chapter 12, Peter Morici, Associate Professor of Government at the University of Maine and an NPA Senior Fellow, looks at the attractions and disadvantages of forming regional trading blocs.

UNDERSTANDING THE ALTERNATIVES

Changes in the international economy since the GATT was formed—the rise of important new trading sectors and the adjustment costs associated with losing, or failing to gain, significant international market shares—have been responsible for creating considerable unrest and disenchantment with the GATT's mechanisms for regulating international trade. Some GATT contracting parties and associated countries have created customs unions and free trade zones that have been inconsistent with the GATT system; the major industrialized nations, however, have generally continued to support the basic principles of the GATT.

We may now be seeing the rise of significant support for managed trade through the use of regional trading blocs as a way to address problems that the GATT has been unable—up to now—to resolve. This study presents the important arguments for and against both regional and multilateral trading systems in an effort to understand the problems of the present system and the alternatives for its future.

Acknowledgments

This book could not have been written without the generous assistance of countless individuals and institutions in North America, Europe and Asia. Although it is not possible to list all of them, we would like to mention at least some.

We would like to thank the International Business Machines Corporation for its active support of this project. This study would not have been possible without IBM's contribution of financial, as well as human, capital. We are also grateful for IBM's encouragement of the National Planning Association's desire to produce a study reflecting many different points of view.

We want to thank the National Planning Association for actively supporting this project. NPA is a unique network of top business, labor, agricultural, professional, and academic leaders. This environment made it possible for us to conduct research and have access to numerous views. We also thank NPA's staff for their support and friendship.

In addition, we are especially grateful to the members of the NPA Advisory Panel on Regional Trading Blocs for their assistance, counsel and critique. Members generously contributed their time and helped to focus our thoughts.

NPA Advisory Panel on Regional Trading Blocs

EDWARD J. CARLOUGH
General President,
Sheet Metal Workers'
International Association

DOMINIQUE CLAVEL
Corporate Senior Vice President,
Chase Manhattan Bank, N.A.

ALAN F. DELP
Senior Vice President,
and Head,
International Banking Group,
First National Bank of Chicago

LODEWIJK J.R. de VINK
Vice President and President,
International Operations,
Warner-Lambert Company

BARBARA J. EASTERLING
Executive Vice President,
Communications Workers of
America

WILLIAM D. EBERLE
President,
Manchester Associates, Ltd.

JOHN H. FALB
Group Executive Vice President,
U.S. and International
Banking Group,
NCNB Texas

THEODORE GEIGER
Distinguished Research Professor of Intersocietal Relations,
School of Foreign Service,
Georgetown University

MELVYN GOETZ
Director of Corporate Development,
Westinghouse Electric Corp.

LAURENCE W. HECHT
Executive Director,
Iacocca Institute,
Lehigh University

ROLF HENEL
President, Lederle International,
American Cyanamid Company

ARTHUR R. LOEVY
Secretary-Treasurer,
Amalgamated Clothing and Textile Workers' Union

WILLIAM R. MILLER
Vice Chairman of the Board,
Bristol-Myers Squibb Company

RUDOLPH A. OSWALD
Director,
Department of Economic Research,
AFL-CIO

HOWARD D. SAMUEL
President,
Industrial Union Department,
AFL-CIO

JOHN A. URQUHART
Senior Vice President,
G.E. Industrial and Power Systems,
General Electric Company

STEPHEN VEHSLAGE
Assistant General Manager of U.S. Education,
IBM United States

The individuals who served on the advisory panel and their organizations did not necessarily agree with all the findings of this study. Many members took exception to various parts. Any errors are those of the authors and not of the panel.

We also wish to thank the members of NPA's Committee on Changing International Realities for their help in providing key direction and suggestions throughout this project.

This book is based on a conference held by NPA on May 1, 1989. We hope that the book presents some of the flavor and excitement of that conference.

Finally, we are grateful to our families for their love, support and guidance—to Paul and to Grace, Joshua and David.

About the Authors

Dr. C. Michael Aho is Director of Economic Studies at the Council on Foreign Relations and a member of NPA's Committee on Changing International Realities.

Mr. Mark Anderson is head of the Office of International Trade and an International Economist in the Department of Economic Research at the AFL-CIO.

Dr. Richard S. Belous is NPA Vice President of International Affairs and a Senior Economist at NPA. He is also the North American Director of the British North-American Committee, which is cosponsored by NPA.

Mr. Michael Calingaert, currently the Director of European Operations at the Pharmaceutical Manufacturers Association in Brussels, was Visiting Senior Fellow at NPA at the time he prepared his chapter.

Dr. Richard V.L. Cooper is the Director of Tax Economics at Price Waterhouse and a member of NPA's Committee on Changing International Realities.

Ms. Maureen A. Farrow is a Partner and Chief Economist for Coopers and Lybrand. She is also a former President of the C.D. Howe Institute in Toronto, Ontario.

Ms. Rebecca S. Hartley is an NPA Fellow in the international program. She has been very active with NPA's Committee on Changing International Realities.

Dr. Peter Morici is Associate Professor of Economics at the University of Maine and an NPA Senior Fellow.

Dr. Dick K. Nanto is a Senior Economist with the Congressional Research Service of the Library of Congress.

Mr. Richard Tropp is the Chief Executive Officer of Washington Development Capital Corporation.

Dr. Herbert E. Weiner is a retired career Foreign Service Officer who is currently a Consultant on labor matters to the Department of State.

Mr. Robert C. York is a Policy Analyst at the C.D. Howe Institute and Canadian Research Director of the Canadian-American Committee, cosponsored by NPA and C.D. Howe.

Regional Trading Blocs: An Introduction

1

by Richard S. Belous and Rebecca S. Hartley

MULTILATERALISM AND REGIONALISM

After World War II, many American government, business and labor leaders placed their faith in a multilateral trading system. Multilateralism describes an open trading system that includes many nations.

Recently, a growing number of public and private sector leaders have been flirting with the notion of regional trading blocs. Regionalism generally refers to the construction of free trade areas, customs unions or sectorial agreements.

The Bretton Woods system, formed at the end of World War II, was envisioned to include the International Monetary Fund, the International Bank for Reconstruction and Development and a multilateral commercial convention. After approval of the IMF and the IBRD, the United States proposed the Havana Charter, which provided for the establishment of the International Trade Organization. The ITO was intended to produce a multilateral framework for international economic relations. But after a three-year delay, the Truman Administration admitted defeat by congressional opposition and decided against submitting the Havana Charter to the Senate for ratification. The General Agreement on Tariffs and Trade, drawn up in 1947 and originally seen as a temporary institution to fill the gap in international trade until the ITO was approved, was made permanent after the failure to ratify the Havana Charter.

The international institutions that reflected the spirit of Bretton Woods were based on the principle of equal rights for each nation, stemming from the assumption of equal burdens. But as Olivier Long, Director General of the GATT from 1968 to 1980, notes, that assumption has changed though the years with the realization that "equality among unequals is inequitable."[1] This change along with the increasing economic pressures on the United States are important factors behind the popularity of regional trading solutions to the United States' trade difficulties.

The term "globalism" is often used in reference to the GATT and its guiding philosophies. But although the GATT has well over 100 contracting parties and associated countries, it still does not include a significant number of nations with centrally planned economies. It also does not provide rules for the regulation of many areas of trade undertaken by the contracting parties. Thus, the GATT is a multilateral rather than a global trading system, even though its members and associates conduct over four-fifths of total world trade.

While the GATT is theoretically based on principles of universality and minimum barriers to the international flow of goods and services, the system was initially made effective through the special role played by the United States in the immediate postwar years. In the late 1940s and early 1950s, the United States maintained a convertible currency and allowed essentially nondiscriminatory access to its enormous domestic market. These practices enabled other countries gradually to liberalize their international trade practices. The postwar period was therefore not an era of pure multilateralism because the degree of a country's adherence to the stated principles of the GATT often depended on that nation's relative competitive strength vis-a-vis the United States.

Through the 1960s, postwar prosperity seemed to reconfirm the initial liberal trade philosophy behind the GATT. But as the growth of the world economy slowed during the 1970s, the consensus on market openness and trade expansion decreased. At the same time, public interest in protectionism—particularly in the United States—increased, and trade politics began to be an important issue in U.S. national elections. The U.S. public has never been particularly interested in, or supportive of, open trade policies.[2] But pressure on Congress to provide import protection for specific sectors increased in the 1970s.

In the 1980s, many Americans came to realize that U.S. dominance of world trade is part of the past. The dual U.S. deficits put pressure on the government to increase U.S. export competitiveness. These changes have, to some degree, resulted in a fascination with managed trade. This neomercantilist-type sentiment has helped erode support for GATT policies and rounds of negotiations. The rise in importance of sectors other than industrial manufacturing has also put pressure on the GATT through the introduction of new mechanisms of protectionism and the increased relevance of nontariff trade barriers. Thus, the GATT has been weakened through the often strong support for sectorial protectionism and the perception that managed trade may be superior to market openness in some cases. A growing interest within the United States in regional trading blocs has resulted.

THE GATT VERSUS REGIONAL TRADING BLOCS

Important differences exist between the principles and characteristics of the GATT and regional trading blocs (see Chart 1.1).

The multilateral GATT system is based on the principle of nondiscrimination. All GATT members are, in theory, bound to grant as favorable treatment to each other as they give to any

CHART 1.1

A COMPARISON OF THE PRINCIPLES AND CHARACTERISTICS OF THE GATT AND THE REGIONAL TRADING BLOC MODEL

GATT Principles and Characteristics	Regional Trading Bloc Principles and Characteristics
(1) Trade is based on the principle of nondiscrimination.	(1) Trade is based on the principle of discrimination.
(2) All members are bound to grant as favorable treatment to each other as they give to any other member, i.e., most-favored-nation status.	(2) Nations within the bloc share special preferences not granted to nations outside the bloc.
(3) To the maximum extent possible, protection should be provided only through tariffs.	(3) Protection is often provided through quantitative restrictions as well as tariffs.
(4) Basic ideas include economic liberalism, multilateralism and free trade based on comparative advantage.	(4) Basic ideas include economic nationalism or regionalism, bilateralism, and trade often based on strategic trade theory and neomercantilism.
(5) The system is designed as a community open to all who are willing to follow membership rules.	(5) The bloc may not be open to all who wish to join and are willing to follow membership rules.
(6) The goal is to build a unified and integrated global system.	(6) The bloc may function as an exclusive club that generates a "them versus us" psychology.
(7) Under Article XXIV, the system provides a three-part test to determine if a regional trading bloc is consistent with the GATT.	(7) In the view of some advocates, blocs are a way of building a stronger multilateral system in the long run.

other country in the application and administration of tariffs and other regulations—the most-favored-nation (MFN) clause of the GATT. Thus, no country may give special trading advantage to another member within the "ideal" GATT framework. However, regional trading blocs are founded on the principle of preferences. In a bloc system, two or more nations may establish a free trade area, a customs union or some form of economic integration. The nations within the bloc have advantages not granted to nations outside the bloc. Hence, regional trading bloc members practice discrimination in granting different preferences to various nations.

A second basic principle of the GATT is that, to the maximum extent possible, protection for domestic industries should be provided only through tariffs. This principle is designed to make the extent of protection clear or, in the language of trade theory, transparent. However, in regional trading blocs, quantitative restrictions or quotas have been used. Thus, supporters of regional trading blocs view managed trade—i.e., trade patterns based on more than short-run supply and demand considerations—as a realistic alternative for solving difficult international trade problems.

GATT supporters tend to base their economic view of the world on the efficacy of free trade and the concept of comparative advantage. Regional trading bloc supporters, although not against free trade in many cases, frequently see a more activist role for the government and other sectors of the economy. They tend to base their economic world view on concepts such as strategic trade—i.e., that trade policies, investment strategies, government activities, and so forth can create or alter a nation's comparative advantage in the global economy—rather than on the traditional concept of free trade.[3]

Perhaps key to the differences between the two trading systems is the "them versus us" psychology underlying regional trading blocs, as opposed to the spirit behind the GATT for a unified, universal trading system.

The ideal GATT and regional trading bloc systems defined above function in an extremely complex world. The GATT has dealt with this real world by establishing "escape clause" regulations that tolerate regional trading blocs in certain cases. Under Article XXIV of the GATT, a regional bloc may be considered consistent with the GATT if the bloc meets a three-part test. First, the bloc or free trade area must include a substantial amount of all the merchandise traded between nations inside the bloc or area. Second, the nations that form the bloc must go through a process of notification with the GATT. Third, the bloc must not be formed to raise new trade barriers to nations outside the bloc. (See Appendix I of this study.)

As required under Article XXIV, the GATT has considered 69 free trade and preferential trade agreements since 1948. (See Appendix II.) However, this GATT-consideration process has left much to be desired. As Jeffrey Schott of the Institute for International Economics notes:

> GATT working parties have reported on each of these arrangements. Only four agreements were deemed to be compatible with Article XXIV requirements; on the other hand, no agreement has been censured as incompatible with GATT rules. . . . As a result, countries have derogated from their MFN obligations with little risk of response from affected third countries.[4]

Because of this situation, some in the international trading community have joked that almost anything can be made "GATT-able." When confronted by a regional trading bloc, the GATT has tended to bend the rules and/or look the other way. In the real world, then, the GATT has coexisted with many regional trading blocs.

THE GROWTH OF REGIONAL TRADING BLOCS

In view of the GATT's Article XXIV escape clause, will more nations try to live within the GATT system and at the same time create new regional trading blocs? Research conducted by the National Planning Association indicates that American executives who are active in international trade believe there will be an increase in regional trading blocs in the future (see Table 1.1). This expectation is based on a survey of U.S. executives who are members of NPA's various committees.[5] These business leaders (mostly executives of Fortune 500 corporations) are involved in many of the strategic decisions that influence their organizations' positions in the international economy. Thus, their views are based on considerable pragmatic day-to-day dealings with the current GATT system.

The majority of the respondents—88 percent—believe that the international trading system is fragmenting and shifting in the direction of more regional trading blocs. It is interesting to note that a majority think the creation of additional blocs will hurt the United States, the world economy and American workers, on balance. However, only a minority believe this shift will hurt their specific organizations, on balance. Thus, most of these executives believe their organizations can somehow obviate most of the costs generated by the growth of regional trading blocs.

The survey also showed that many of the executives think the United States should sign new free trade agreements with a

TABLE 1.1

EXPECTATIONS OF U.S. EXECUTIVES IN THE AREA OF INTERNATIONAL TRADE

Statement	Percent of U.S. Executives Who Agree
(1) The world economy is shifting in the direction of more regional trading blocs, e.g., the United States and Canada, the European Community, and Japan and Asia.	88%
(2) A shift to an increased role for regional trading blocs would hurt the United States.	77
(3) A shift to an increased role for regional trading blocs would hurt the world economy.	63
(4) A shift to an increased role for regional trading blocs would hurt my organization, on balance.	42
(5) A shift to an increased role for regional trading blocs would hurt the current round of GATT talks, on balance.	75
(6) A shift to an increased role for regional trading blocs would hurt American workers, on balance.	64
(7) I believe that most of the NIEs would rather form a regional trading bloc with the United States than with Japan.	69
(8) The United States should sign free trade agreements with:	
a. Mexico	63
b. Japan	41
c. one or all of the NIEs	40
d. the European Community	53
e. other countries and/or regions	18
(9) My organization has altered its business strategy in a specific way because of expectations of growing regional trading blocs.	37

Source: Estimates based on 1989 NPA survey data.

number of countries. A U.S.-Mexico free trade agreement is favored by 63 percent, with the next most popular FTA candidate being the European Community (53 percent).

Therefore, based on NPA survey data, two conclusions can be reached:

(1) many American executives expect to see the role of regional trading blocs increase in the global economy; and

(2) many American executives believe the growth of regional trading blocs could weaken the current GATT system.

CONVENTIONAL ANALYSIS

It is important to understand the potential impact the growth of regional trading blocs could have on the world economy. The conventional analysis of regional trading blocs, free trade agreements, customs unions, and so forth is often based on the seminal work of economist Jacob Viner.[6] By using the Viner model, numerous economists, policymakers and business leaders view a multilateral international trading system, such as the GATT, as a "best" solution; use of the Viner model also shows why trade experts often point to regional trading blocs as being a "second-best" solution.

Viner looked at trade creation and trade diversion. Trade creation occurs when new opportunities for free trade are opened up. As trade creation increases, consumers, companies and governments have a greater chance of giving their business to the most efficient producer of a specific good or service. Conversely, trade diversion results when free trade is restricted. Consumers, companies and governments in a system fostering trade diversion do not always have an opportunity to use the most efficient producer of a specific good or service.

When a multilateral system like the GATT is expanded, the net result is growth in trade creation, which is viewed by most trade experts as beneficial for all members of the trading system. However, when a regional trading bloc is formed, the net result is a combination of trade creation—a benefit—and trade diversion—a cost. If a regional trading bloc results in considerable trade diversion, many costs are placed on the world trading system.

Consider, for example, the United States, Canada and the United Kingdom. Suppose the most efficient producer of a specific good is the United Kingdom. If the multilateral trading system is healthy, consumers in the United States and Canada would probably have the opportunity to purchase needed parts from British suppliers. This would be an example of trade creation. Suppose the United States and Canada form a regional trading bloc. Many experts argue that the new U.S.-Canada Free Trade

Agreement represents a trading bloc. Under trade diversion, American consumers might purchase the product from Canadian suppliers even though British producers might be the best source for the good. The reason for such trade diversion could be reduced tariffs between the United States and Canada, while tariffs between North America and the United Kingdom remain the same.

An expanded multilateral system that results in increased trade creation—and no trade diversion—is viewed by many trade experts as the best policy option. Because regional trading blocs generate trade diversion as well as trade creation, many experts see blocs as an inferior alternative to expanding the GATT system to cover more issues and to include more signatories. But a problem arises in trying to fit conventional trade theory to the real world. The GATT simply may not soon cover many explosive trade issues. The trick will be to reconcile theory with reality.

THE LOSS OF FAITH IN THE GATT

While a growing number of trade experts might agree in theory with the discussion above, concern is increasing about the ability of the GATT to deal with several new international realities. Furthermore, some analysts and business and labor leaders point out that trade diversion and trade creation are only part of the total picture. Although an improved GATT system might be the first choice of many in the international trading community, many business, labor and political leaders have lost faith in the GATT and are turning to regional trading blocs as realistic "second-best" policy options.

What has caused the diminished trust in the GATT? A model of the international system constructed by Theodore Geiger of Georgetown University indicates why many U.S. business and labor leaders are looking to alternative international trading systems. Built on the international "leadership" model of Charles Kindleberger, the Geiger paradigm moves beyond the standard trade creation and trade diversion type of analysis.[7]

A central feature of the Geiger hypothesis is that the GATT was and is in many ways a reflection of the United States' value and preference systems. According to Geiger, in the post-World War II era, the United States and the Soviet Union became hegemonic leaders of the two major world blocs. He points out:

> The kind and degree of international economic integration established during the postwar period would not have been achieved without the strong insistence of the United States on moving steadily toward the goal and the ideas it generated for doing so. Left to their own inclinations, the West European countries and other OECD nations would have re-

> constructed a system with a substantially lower level of integration. As they did during the interwar period, they would very probably have retained protection for . . . domestic producers. . . . The actions of the United States were crucial in the formation of a multilateral, nondiscriminatory, increasingly competitive, and freely trading international economic system in those years.[8]

This multilateral system provided numerous benefits for all the nations who joined the GATT. In the 1950s and 1960s, the international system experienced a period of rapid economic growth, high productivity levels and increases in standards of living. But the GATT system also generated problems for member countries in the form of adjustment costs. As the hegemonic leader, the United States was willing to absorb more than its share of these costs (which often took the form of job displacement and/or increased American market shares going to foreign producers) for a number of reasons.

First, the United States felt a responsibility to help European and Asian nations get back on their feet after World War II. The United States also felt it should play a leading role in helping the developing nations, and this assistance often took the form of increased access to the American market and financial support. Third, the U.S. economy was so strong and dynamic after World War II that it was relatively easy for the country to pay these adjustment costs. Furthermore, international trade represented a smaller part of America's gross national product compared to other nations, so adjustment costs were not as onerous. Fifth, the prize of easy access to the massive U.S. market was one way the United States maintained its hegemonic leadership within the free world. Finally, by having a more open market than its trading partners, America demonstrated that its leaders were serious about their multilateral, free trade values.

The rounds of GATT reform that reduced tariff levels were dependent upon American leadership. However, as Geiger notes, in the 1970s and 1980s, the United States' role in the international system was somewhat reduced, and the United States has often been unable to act as a hegemonic leader in terms of economic power.

Asian and European government, business and labor leaders—as well as the American public—have never shared the relatively strong multilateral, free trade ideology of many U.S. public and private sector decisionmakers. Thus, with the U.S. decline as an undisputed hegemonic leader has come a weakening of the foundation upon which the GATT was built and a decline of multilateral, free trade values.

Compared to the 1950s and 1960s, the international system of the 1970s and 1980s saw lower productivity and real income growth rates. In this era of slow or no growth, the relative role of the international trading sector has expanded in the American economy. Hence, any relative level of international shock results in a higher level of impact within the United States. The adjustment costs associated with the GATT have become much larger in recent years, and when push comes to shove, few political leaders are willing to pay those costs.

Because of the higher adjustment costs and the United States' decline in relative standing in the world economy, many political, business and labor leaders have sought alternatives to the GATT system. While they may still publicly support the GATT (and fervently hope for a reformed multilateral system) a growing number of public and private sector leaders are hedging their bets through means such as bilateral agreements, free trade zones and customs unions.

The GATT is also currently facing difficult nontariff barrier issues. Although it may have been relatively easy to reduce tariffs, it is much more difficult to hammer out common rules for issues such as intellectual property rights and government procurement procedures. In addition, it is proving difficult to expand the GATT system to cover areas like international trade in agriculture and services. Finally, more and more American business, government and labor leaders have come to view the GATT as a very weak system with slow enforcement of trading rules.

A QUICK AND EASY SOLUTION

Compared to the difficulty of reforming the GATT, a regional trading bloc appears to be a quick and easy solution to international trade problems. It is often much easier to negotiate a bilateral agreement than a multilateral one. If some nations will not agree to expand the GATT to include, for example, trade in services, some trade experts argue that America should sign "little GATTs" with nations that do agree.

Still other experts have pointed out that the parents of the GATT were several bilateral agreements.[9] They argue that just as bilateral agreements were expanded to form the GATT, new bilateral deals could be used to reform the GATT and that the road to a stronger multilateral system may be through regional trading blocs. The United States should thus continue to espouse an expanded multilateral system; however, it should also sign more regional trading bloc agreements or use the threat of more regional deals to push forward GATT reforms.

There are problems with this quick and easy solution. It is not at all clear that a series of regional agreements could help build a unified multilateral system. Furthermore, the multilateral system may not be strong enough to withstand the pressures of an increased system of regional trading blocs. A real concern is that this American tactic, instead of being a kick in the pants for the GATT, could wind up being a shot in the heart.

GROWING NEOMERCANTILISM

In view of the problems discussed above and the long-term trade deficits experienced by the United States and other nations, the near-term future for the international trading system may not hold expanded multilateral free trade. The trends shaping the future of the international system may be more in the direction of neomercantilism. As Geiger points out:

> This concept encompasses many other important phenomena in addition to what is conventionally known as "protectionism," that is, the imposition of barriers to prevent or reduce the entry of competing foreign goods and services into a country. By analogy with the mercantilism that shaped the policies of the European states in the 17th and 18th centuries, I define the neomercantilist trend as the increasing determination of a nation's economic activities . . . by nonefficiency criteria rather than by market forces. . . . Hitherto, neomercantilism has mainly been manifested in trade relationships, where the high level of integration attained by the end of the postwar period has gradually been eroding.[10]

The current interest in regional trading blocs as a potential solution to various international economic problems has been bolstered by recent developments in economic thought.

As noted, a reformed GATT—based on the concepts of multilateralism, free trade and comparative advantage—has been the first choice of most leading economic thinkers in the United States. Most of the arguments against free trade and comparative advantage can be dismissed easily.[11] For this reason, the concepts of neomercantilism and regional trading blocs have not been supported by the majority of leading American economists.

However, occasionally a new economic concept is presented that makes even ardent free trade advocates take notice. The so-called infant industry case has long been recognized by most free trade supporters as valid in theory. The argument is that it may be rational for a nation to protect an infant industry from global competition. Once that industry grows up, the nation can end protection and let the industry compete in global markets. However, in the real world, there have been numerous complications with this theory, and many nations have been stuck protecting infants that never grew up.

The so-called Keynesian case also has been acknowledged by many free trade backers as a valid concept. As Keynes explained during the Great Depression, free trade analysis often assumes a world of full employment. If significant unemployment exists and if resources (including labor) lack perfect mobility, then expansion of free trade can cause numerous problems for an economy. In recognition of the Keynesian case, most modern free trade advocates now support various programs to aid those hurt by the expansion of international competition.

While mercantilism is often presented as a bad idea, it is interesting to note that Keynes—among others—had some kind things to say about it. For example, Keynes noted in his *General Theory* that there was an:

> element of scientific truth in mercantilist doctrine. . . . Mercantilist thought never supposed that there was a self-adjusting tendency by which the rate of interest would be established at the appropriate level. . . . The mercantilists were aware of the fallacy of cheapness and the danger that excessive competition may turn the terms of trade against a country. . . . The mercantilists were under no illusions as to the nationalistic character of their policies. . . . It was national advantage and relative strength at which they were admittedly aiming.[12]

It would not be surprising to see neomercantilist sentiments play a larger role in the construction of American trade policy if the U.S. trade deficit is not reduced. Although the advocates of multilateralism and free trade still represent the majority point of view among American economic thinkers, this view—the foundation of the GATT system—is now under serious attack.

STRATEGIC TRADE THEORY

Advocates of strategic trade question the traditional concept of comparative advantage. They point out that the traditional multilateral, free trade and comparative advantage models have been built on the assumption of perfect competition. However, for many key international industries—such as computers, aerospace, automobiles, telecommunications, banking, insurance, and pharmaceuticals—the assumption of perfect competition may be far from accurate. Instead, these industries may be more oligopolies or quasi-monopolies.

For example, the international market may be able to support only two supercomputer producers in the long run. If the successful supercomputer firms are Japanese and European, American consumers of the product could pay excess profits (or, in the language of economists, economic rents) to the Japanese and European firms. The American economy could thus be hurt: economic rents would be flowing into the Japanese and European economies, and U.S. firms could be locked out of a growing market and technological area.

Advocates of this theory also note that various strategies, including the targeting of American industries, have worked for the Japanese and others. Advocates further point out that comparative advantage can be altered by a nation's public and private sectors and by public-private partnerships and joint efforts.[13] For example, they note that the strong U.S. position in aerospace exports might be due in part to historic government support of this industry.

While recognizing that strategic trade supporters have made several interesting points in theory, free trade backers insist that, given political realities and the complexities of the international trading system, it will be very hard for governments to carry out sound strategic policies. They argue that, in the long run, it will be impossible for government policymakers to make sounder decisions than those resulting from free market forces.

FREE RIDERS

Advocates of expanded multilateralism note that the GATT system functions in part like a public good in providing benefits for all members, even those that do not take significant steps toward trade liberalization. As standard economic theory recognizes, there is a "free rider" aspect associated with all public goods. If some individuals or countries receive a benefit regardless of paying for that benefit, then they behave as free riders. The GATT system does have cases of conditional benefits, which can be enjoyed only by a nation that contributes toward trade liberalization. However, the GATT must still deal with the free rider issue.

A regional trading bloc agreement can obviate the public goods problem. Because these agreements are built on the concept of preferences and discrimination, a potential free rider can be excluded from the agreement. This type of solution is obviously attractive to U.S. policymakers who feel the United States has shouldered too much of the burden of a multilateral system for too long.

TWO-TIERED POLICIES

Future trends on the international trading front will likely continue to be quite complex. Most successful political leaders place little value on ideological purity and, in fact, govern by convincing often conflicting forces to live inside the same tent. In the area of international trade, Western political leaders may be able to do this by creating two-tiered trading policies. To understand what is meant by a two-tiered trading system, it is useful to review the three ideologies of political economy used by Robert Gilpin of Princeton University in his model of international relations. As Gilpin notes:

> Economic liberalism, Marxism, and economic nationalism are all very much alive at the end of the twentieth century; they define the conflicting perspectives that individuals have with regard to the implications of the market system for domestic and international society. Many of the issues that were controversial in the eighteenth and nineteenth centuries are once again being intensely debated.[14]

The Liberal perspective on political economy is based on the foundations of classical economics as developed in Great Britain, the United States and parts of Western Europe. From Adam Smith to the University of Chicago, the liberal perspective assumes that "a market arises spontaneously in order to satisfy human needs and that, once it is in operation, it functions in accordance with its own internal logic."[15] This perspective believes the market system and free trade create the conditions for solid economic growth, economic efficiency and individual liberty.

The Nationalist perspective includes "a set of themes or attitudes rather than a coherent and systematic body of economic or political theory."[16] The main idea is that economic activities should be directed toward the enhancement of a national objective. "Economic nationalists stress the role of economic factors in international relations, and view the struggle among states . . . for economic resources as pervasive and indeed inherent in the nature of the international system itself," Gilpin states.[17]

The Marxist perspective will not be part of the two-tiered trend that we envision Western policymakers adopting.

What we have called a two-tiered international trading policy incorporates aspects from both the Liberal and Nationalist perspectives. To retain power and hold conflicting coalition partners together, successful political leaders must be able to combine both perspectives. In many cases the mix will not be clean, and the policy will often contain major contradictions. But the mix will be necessary to hold opposing forces within the same political coalition.

The "them versus us" psychology of regional trading blocs could become quite evident in a two-tiered trading policy. Within the bloc, the Liberal perspective could be allowed to increase and grow. But outside the bloc, the Nationalist, or regional, perspective could become the major point of view. If other nations refuse to play by the Liberal perspective's rules, then the political leaders who consider themselves to be the sons and daughters of the Liberal perspective may have to develop two-tiered policies.

THE IMPACT OF TWO-TIERED POLICIES ON THE GATT

If extensive two-tiered policies are adopted by the United States, they will damage the GATT. Any significant defection of the United States from the GATT would be crippling to that system.

The GATT is an unusual international organization because it is contractual. The system has worked well in the past because the contracting parties have realized that its rules and principles benefited them. Since the GATT was established in 1948, the volume of world trade has increased approximately tenfold. Contracting parties to the GATT now number 97, and associated countries, more than 120.[18]

In general, the GATT has been quite successful in dealing with trade issues that are clearly defined and that are perceived as serious by the most influential contracting countries. However, within the United States and between these influential contracting parties, the political consensus in favor of trade liberalization has been decreasing. More and more the viewpoint is heard that exports are the benefit of trade and imports are the cost.

I.M. Destler of the Institute for International Economics has identified a significant degree of antiprotectionist sentiment in the United States, which he believes may help stem the erosion of U.S. public support for the GATT. But he cautions that the political pressure for antiprotectionist policies is often not as strong as the pressure for existing protectionism.[19] Public antiprotectionist forces are not easy to organize and in any event will probably not present much of a barrier to an extensive two-tiered system if the U.S. trade deficit continues to be so large.

Traditionally, the GATT has dealt well with problems of overt restrictions. These restrictions are usually imposed at a border on goods that are exchanged as a result of contracts between businesses in countries that have market economies. However, the GATT has dealt poorly with more esoteric problems such as the issues of government intervention through domestic assistance programs and benefits accruing to businesses due to a government's explicit or implicit industrial policy. Either such problems were not present immediately after World War II, or the United States ignored their existence because they did not impose unacceptable adjustment costs. More recently, these issues have resulted in a modification of the GATT principle of nondiscrimination, especially as less developed countries (LDCs) have increasingly become contracting parties or associated countries.

Will further modifications of the GATT through the use of Article XXIV substantially replace the GATT with a system of regional trading blocs? Probably not, unless the United States and Canada as well as the European Community create free trade agreements that are not GATT-consistent. It has long been overlooked that many of the LDC trading blocs are inconsistent with GATT Article XXIV because they do not "include a plan and schedule for the formation of . . . a customs union or . . . free trade area within a reasonable length of time."[20] Such free trade areas are often not officially recognized by the GATT; they are formed and lapse in relative obscurity. Although these unions may be created with the intent of protecting markets as well as expanding trade, it is generally not worthwhile for the developed nations to bring objections concerning them to the GATT. Such unions and free trade areas do not pose a threat to the GATT. However, if the developed nations endeavored to form exclusive, market-protecting FTAs that were not designed in the spirit of the GATT, significant damage to the spirit and institutions of the GATT would arise.

THE IMPACT OF REGIONAL TRADING BLOCS

Policy Implications for the United States

The United States, despite its decreasing share of world trade, cannot afford a significant dismantling of the GATT system or its institutions. It cannot continue to serve as the primary market for LDC imports. It cannot ignore domestic pressures for improving its balance of trade. These pressures seem to point the United States toward different international trading policies. In reality, however, they point the United States toward a three-pronged agenda for reform of the international system and of some of its domestic policies. The broad areas in need of reform measures are:

- the GATT institutional framework and bureaucracy;
- the U.S. trade bureaucracy system; and
- U.S. industry and the educational system.

Admittedly, these are extremely broad categories, but substantial changes must be made in each area to effect a lasting improvement in the United States' position in international trade.

In the GATT negotiations, the United States should continue to try to be a consensus-builder, recognizing the decline in its hegemonic leadership in the international trade arena. It is possible that this implicit U.S. leadership role will have to be replaced by a strengthened GATT system for the GATT to regain the influence it exerted prior to 1970. Extensive reform of the GATT—such as envisioned by Jan Tumlir, a GATT researcher[21]—would necessitate firm, insightful guidance by the major signatories, traits lacking in the GATT leadership in recent years.

The Bush Administration does not appear committed to taking the politically difficult step of allowing GATT bodies to rule on U.S. trading policy. If America is no longer committed to its role as the leader of a free trade system regardless of adjustment costs, another power must assume this position or the multilateral system will eventually become useless for trade regulation.

As noted above, a strengthened GATT system might be able to fill the gap left by the United States. But if the United States does not appear to take GATT rulings seriously, this solution could be undermined. For example, in October 1989, Rufus Yerxa, U.S. Deputy Trade Representative, refused for the seventh time to allow the GATT Council to adopt a disputes panel recommendation that the United States change how its courts handle patent infringement cases involving imports. U.S. trading partners frequently perceive the United States as ready to act unilaterally on its own interpretations of its trading partners' contraventions of the GATT, but as unwilling to accept GATT rulings against its own contraventions.[22] For the United States to help strengthen GATT institutions, it will have to accept some limits on its sovereignty, such as those recommended by GATT disputes panels.

In addition, if the United States is to help extend GATT coverage to sectors and issues such as intellectual property rights that are not presently addressed, it must have the cooperation of other major contracting parties. Because the consequences of adjustments to fluctuations in international trade are great, the United States can no longer afford to stand alone on many of the issues, providing unlimited access to its markets as an incentive for even the less than full cooperation of others.

Systemic Problems and Adjustment Implications

There has been a trend toward interventionist trade policies in Congress.[23] The development of at least a two-tiered system—or a reformed multilateral system—is vital if the creation of U.S. trade policy is not to become a morass. If managed trade becomes the dominant force behind U.S. trade policy, Congress will be ill-equipped to resist constituent demands for sectorial import protection.

The executive branch needs to maintain its role as trade policy leader. The Bush Administration was extremely laggard in appointing subcabinet level officials in agencies concerned with trade issues. This resulted in giving both Congress and U.S. foreign trading partners the initiative in setting the U.S. foreign trade agenda. (Congressional staffs, for their part, are not large enough to conduct a managed trade policy on a global level.) Continued emphasis on a multilateral approach will do much to strengthen the executive branch's role in trade policy determination.

As discussed below, the United States is having to accept loss of dominance in international markets as well as in some sectors of its domestic market. But the American public will continue to be concerned about foreign trade to the extent that it directly affects American jobs. Therefore, the United States may find that an improved adjustment assistance program is the price of maintaining public and congressional support for a multilateral approach to the world trading system.

Human Resource Implications

The impact of regional trading blocs is most often assessed in the product market sector of the economy. For example, what will be the net results for computer sales or for automotive market shares? However, regional trading blocs can have a major impact on labor markets and social policy as well.

A trading bloc can provide management with many additional options in terms of plant location, compensation structures and employment patterns. A bloc can influence management's position toward unions. Econometric studies often conclude that the formation of a regional trading bloc will have little impact on a nation's unemployment rate. But such trade agreements can influence the pattern of labor-management relations in a nation. Changes on the international trading front have already become a new "wild card" in labor-management relations, and labor is starting to respond to these shifting conditions. In the European Community, for example, labor is taking an active role in the formation of European labor market standards and social policies.

COMING TO TERMS WITH THE GLOBAL ECONOMY

The United States must accept the reality that it is no longer the hegemonic leader of the West. U.S. goods are no longer the best in some sectors, and the nation must learn how to compete in a global economy that does not trade solely in tangible goods. Some U.S. business and labor leaders have faced the fact of increasing foreign competition and are already adapting, sometimes by using foreign techniques that have proven effective. The larger challenge will be to encourage others to follow this lead.

The United States should guard against the overuse of policies such as voluntary restraint agreements to protect certain sectors' domestic markets from foreign competition. VRAs are an example of GATT-circumventing behavior that weakens the multilateral approach and the credibility of the GATT to deal with difficult issues.

Rather than depend on such short-range policies, the U.S. government should plan ahead to strengthen the U.S. educational system as well as business competitiveness. It would be folly to try to paste together a coherent international trading system from piecemeal protectionism.

That the U.S. share of world trade and influence is not at the level it was during the heyday of the GATT is not in itself a catastrophe. The United States still has the world's largest economy and domestic market. But it is becoming more dependent on international trade and cannot prosper by simply protecting and supplying its domestic market. The United States must make the adjustments necessary for trading in a diverse and more equally balanced world economy, or it will be ill-equipped to weather the next recession. While the United States may no longer be an undisputed hegemonic leader, it is still the coalition leader of the Western trading partnership. This new leadership role as a "first among equals" continues to make U.S. actions in the international trading system extremely important for that system's future.

RESPONSIBILITY SHARING IN INTERNATIONAL TRADE

The true test of an international trading system is not how it functions in the best of times, but how it functions in a serious recession. An international trading system based on bilateral agreements will not work in the event of a major recession; a world fragmented into regional trading blocs cannot cope with the pressures generated by bad times.

The 1930s saw the growth of so-called coprosperity spheres based on bilateral agreements. Each trading bloc looked out only for its own interests, and no nation was concerned about the effects on the system as a whole. As in the complex U.S. financial system, the international trading system often needs a "lender of last resort" as a stabilizer in difficult times. The bilateral or regional trade route does not provide such a stabilizer; indeed, the negative experience of coprosperity spheres led directly to the initiation of the multilateral approach after World War II.

A bilateral agreement or a regional trading bloc is like a club that emphasizes the exclusion of others. A multilateral agreement resembles a community that is open to all who are willing to follow a few basic rules. The United States, we believe, should invest its political capital in fostering an international trading community rather than seeking the short-run benefits generated by exclusive clubs.

But the United States cannot be expected to absorb a larger share of the adjustment costs generated by multilateralism and business cycles. The multilateral system will have to devise ways of dealing with adjustment costs other than tariffs and nontariff trade barriers. The concept of burden sharing is often mentioned in the context of military defense. International trade faces a similar, and difficult, burden sharing—we call it responsibility sharing—issue.

Since World War II, the United States has been the primary force and spirit behind the GATT. If the United States moves in the direction of more bilateral and regional agreements, the rest of the world will follow that example. If the United States places significant emphasis on regional agreements, the GATT system will be seriously damaged. The United States, like other nations, will probably have to develop a two-tiered trading policy that includes regionalism and multilateralism. Our hope is that multilateralism does not suffer in the process.

NOTES

1. Olivier Long, *Law and Its Limitations in the GATT Multilateral Trade System* (Dordrecht, the Netherlands: Martinus Nijhoff Publishers, 1987), p. 5.
2. I.M. Destler, *American Trade Politics: System Under Stress* (Washington, D.C.: Institute for International Economics, 1986), p. 149.
3. Marc Levinson, "Is Strategic Trade Fair Trade?" *Across the Board* (June 1988), pp. 47-51.
4. Jeffrey J. Schott, "More Free Trade Areas?" in *Free Trade Areas and U.S. Trade Policy*, ed. Jeffrey J. Schott (Washington, D.C.: Institute for International Economics, 1989), pp. 24-25.
5. The National Planning Association has five policy and research committees: the British-North American Committee, the Committee on Changing International Realities, the Canadian-American Committee, the Food and Agriculture Committee, and the Committee on New American Realities. The 480 members of these committees include top business, labor, academic, and professional leaders.
6. Jacob Viner, *The Customs Union Issue* (New York: Carnegie Endowment for International Peace, 1953); see also Charles P. Kindleberger, *International Economics* (Homewood, Ill.: Richard D. Irwin, Inc., 1968), pp. 183-218.
7. For more on these "leadership" models, see Theodore Geiger, *The Future of the International System: The United States and the World Political Economy* (Boston: Unwin Hyman, 1988); and Charles P. Kindleberger, *The World in Depression: 1929-1939* (Berkeley: University of California Press, 1973).
8. Geiger, *The Future*, p. 11.

9. William Diebold, Jr., "The History of the Issue," in *Bilateralism, Multilateralism and Canada in U.S. Trade Policy*, ed. William Diebold, Jr. (Cambridge, Mass.: Ballinger Publishing Co., 1988), pp. 1-16.
10. Geiger, *The Future*, pp. 101, 103.
11. For an example of how leading American economists have dismissed most of the arguments against free trade based on comparative advantage, see Paul A. Samuelson and William D. Nordhaus, *Economics* (New York: McGraw-Hill Book Co., 1985), pp. 831-868.
12. John Maynard Keynes, *The General Theory of Employment, Interest, and Money* (New York: Harcourt, Brace and World, Inc., 1965), pp. 335, 341, 345, 348.
13. Bruce R. Scott, "National Strategies: Key to International Competition," in *U.S. Competitiveness in the World Economy*, ed. Bruce R. Scott and George C. Lodge (Boston: Harvard Business School Press, 1985), pp. 71-143; see also Michael E. Porter, *Competitive Strategy: Techniques for Analyzing Industries and Competitors* (New York: Free Press, 1980), pp. 287-298.
14. Robert Gilpin, *The Political Economy of International Relations* (Princeton: Princeton University Press, 1987), pp. 25-26.
15. Ibid., pp. 27-28.
16. Ibid., p. 31.
17. Ibid., p. 32.
18. Long, *Law and Its Limitations*, p. 5.
19. I.M. Destler and John S. Odell, "Anti-Protection: Changing Forces in United States Trade Policy," *Policy Analyses in International Economics* (Washington, D.C.: Institute for International Economics, September 1987), p. 139.
20. GATT, Part III, Article XXIV, Section 5c.
21. Jan Tumlir, "International Economic Order: Can the Trend Be Reversed?" *The World Economy* (March 1982).
22. William Dullforce, "Concern Rises at GATT over US Double Standards," *The Financial Times* (October 20, 1989), p. 3.
23. Destler, *American Trade Politics*.

A Recipe for RIBS—
Resentment, Inefficiency, Bureaucracy, and Stupid Signals

by C. Michael Aho

SIX UNKNOWNS

In looking at the current world trading system, there are at least six key unknowns. One, of course, is the U.S.-Canada Free Trade Agreement, a historic accord that began to be implemented at the start of 1989. The second unknown is the European plan to form a unified internal market by 1992. It has been referred to by some as the "infernal internal market." How this process develops in the next few years will be both interesting and significant. The third unknown is the new U.S. trade bill, referred to by some as the "ominous omnibus trade bill," and its implementation.

The multilateral trade talks known as the Uruguay Round are the fourth unknown. Interest in the Uruguay Round, which could alter the General Agreement on Tariffs and Trade, varies almost from day to day and according to which country one is in and with whom one speaks. For example, consider the Uruguay Round vis-a-vis Europe 1992. Europeans are able to relate specific plans and programs and explain how the new market will influence their countries and their lives. But when asked what the Uruguay Round is, they are likely to respond, "What's that—a new form of sausage?" The lack of European interest in the multilateral trade negotiations will be a problem in trying to move forward on the GATT negotiations.

The fifth unknown is the business cycle. Depending upon whether the world economy is in a slump or a boom, the U.S.-Canada FTA or EC 1992 could look very different to private and public sector decisionmakers. The sixth key unknown involves the recent dramatic shifts in Eastern Europe and their impact on both the communist and Western nations.

The potential trend toward bilateral or regional trading blocs troubles many observers. Such blocs create uncertainty and disrupt plans for the growing number of businesses that depend on international markets. Furthermore, a trend toward regional blocs would greatly alter the current multilateral trading system. The multilateral talks are, in this author's view, the best solution to the current problems facing the world trading system. My basic thesis is that the actions of the United States in the 1990s will be the key to determining whether world trade develops in the direction of more regional trading blocs or toward a reformed multilateral system.

THE U.S.-CANADA FTA: A CRITICAL INDICATOR

Although the U.S.-Canada FTA and the forces behind the Europe 1992 program evolved from entirely different circumstances, their simultaneity has raised the issue of whether we are moving toward a new system of increased regional trading blocs. Moreover, many U.S. decisionmakers are considering whether America should—or could—replicate the FTA elsewhere in the world.

As an economist who has given the Reagan Administration little credit for anything in the area of international trade policy, I acknowledge that it deserves the credit for negotiating the United State's historic agreement with Canada. The FTA went further, faster, than the multilateral trade talks, and it could be a catalyst to the Uruguay Round. In addition, the agreement demonstrates that trade liberalization is still possible, and it helps to make a credible case to Congress that international negotiations can continue to bear fruit.

But before the United States attempts to replicate that agreement, it should take stock of the FTA. Despite the vast similarities in both nations' legal and business environments, the FTA is a complex international deal. Moreover, the signing of the agreement was not the end of the process, but only the beginning.

The future holds many questions for FTA-related cases. How durable will the agreement be? How will the elaborate binational dispute settling mechanism work, and how much credibility should it be given? How will the unaddressed issues involving individual service sectors be resolved? What will happen in the area of subsidies where America and Canada were unable to complete an agreement? How will this new bilateral agreement mesh with the multilateral talks? Since neither country put everything on the table during the FTA negotiations because of the concurrent multilateral talks, will Canada or the United States seek to recontract if the talks prove unfruitful in certain areas? Also, how will the United States and Canada respond to changing circumstances generated, say, by Europe 1992? While a common U.S.-Canada position on EC 1992 policies may be possible, Canada would probably not be enthusiastic if, for example, the EC and the United States were to cut a deal on the Common Agricultural Policy.

Thus, as we move into the 1990s, a prime issue concerns how the U.S.-Canada FTA will evolve, especially in terms of third country issues. America already has a so-called framework agreement with Mexico, and there is talk about moving a little further, for instance, by starting sectorial talks with Mexico. Because of the overlap of trade between the North American countries in areas such as auto parts, energy and numerous other goods, Canada would probably want to have considerable input before the United States expands negotiations with Mexico.

The U.S.-Canada FTA is a good agreement; still, it does not address some of the central trade difficulties between the two countries, such as subsidies, intellectual property rights and agricultural issues. It has other deficiencies as well, including the omission of some key trading areas. Thus, before launching another bilateral round of negotiations, it would be best to see how the U.S.-Canada FTA works out before opening negotiations with, say, Japan.

THE PROBLEMS OF RIBS

Bilateral free trade agreements are justified only in specific cases. Israel (for political reasons) and Canada (for reasons of proximity and interdependence) are very special cases. The EC, in its own way, is also a special case. President Reagan spoke of including Mexico in a North American accord, and a U.S.-Mexico FTA may also be a special case. But beyond these, it would not be healthy for the world trading system if the United States were to take the bilateral path.

Bluntly put, a series of regional trading blocs would be a recipe for "RIBS," that is, resentment, inefficiency, bureaucracy, and stupid signals.

Resentment would be spawned among outsiders. Inefficiency would result from the fragmentation of markets, creating more uncertainty for businesses that operate on a global basis. Bureaucracy would increase because governments and businesses would feel obligated to discover whether countries or blocs had discriminatory policies that affected them. Finally, more regional blocs would send stupid, or at least silly, signals to developing country friends who are proponents of market-oriented solutions and multilateralism.

For the United States to look beyond Canada, Israel and perhaps Mexico in terms of regional agreements would be a big mistake. Discriminatory bilateral agreements are not building blocks that can be stacked to create a stable multinational trading system. No one could put them all together.

In the first place, the expectations that are engendered by already existing regional trading agreements would be undermined. Much of the momentum behind the U.S.-Canada FTA came from business. How will corporations respond if their expectations are not fulfilled? For example, suppose the United States formed an FTA with Mexico. On the basis of the new U.S.-Canada FTA, Canadian and American businesses are planning their strategies, and they may be reallocating their resources, investments and so forth. With Mexico in the picture, executives in the auto parts industry in Canada would certainly ask, "What happened to our special deal? We had expectations of preferential access to the United States. Now there is a third country that might start supplying the U.S. market duty free." The business community needs time to work with the U.S.-Canada FTA before having to deal with further bilateral arrangements.

Another problem area involves Congress, which must approve any additional bilateral free trade agreements. There is a strong domestic political aspect to the formation of bilateral pacts. If America starts forming other pacts or disaggregating trade according to sectorial interests, members of Congress would get whipsawed by various foreign interests. Many of the congressional leaders and staff that I have been associated with prefer not to be involved in the micromanagement of international trade policy. They dislike the job of having to decide what countries the United States should discriminate against and what sectors should be hurt.

Of course, legislative action and separate regional or bilateral agreements also raise the possibility that trade policy could become a higher form of foreign policy. Someone on Capitol Hill will probably say, "If we start forming other bilateral pacts, perhaps we should link trade talks with our political and military objectives. For example, maybe we ought to pull the trade plug on a country if it does not reflect our political or military policies." Were this scenario to become reality, international trade would become high foreign policy, and our current Secretary of State (who was an early proponent of more bilateral trade agreements) would find himself spending more time on the balance of international trade than on weapons reduction policies. This would also leave him less time to spend on increasingly important issues such as the balance of terror.

In addition to the political and economic arguments and any inefficiencies created by regional trading blocs, a crucial problem would be the fragmented global trading system. How would the indebted developing countries (or the United States, for that matter) manage to generate a trade surplus that would allow them to service their mounting foreign debt? What would happen to the dynamism that we have seen in the Far East if rival trading blocs arise and create considerable interbloc uncertainty and friction?

PLAYING FAVORITES

At the political level, the essence of regional trading blocs is playing favorites. This creates foreign policy problems with those left out. Thus, in addition to domestic political problems, a misguided regional trading bloc strategy could alter the contours of political and military alliances. As noted above, Congress would be under intense pressure to withdraw trade preferences, or withhold further liberalization, if countries were deemed to be acting inconsistently with U.S. foreign policy objectives. Do members of Congress want to get involved in such detailed decisions? Probably not. Congress is not likely to have the political will or the time and resources to review, oversee and legislate a series of regional trading bloc agreements with all the attendant political pressures that would entail.

Despite the problems discussed above, there is serious interest in more FTAs and sectorial agreements. The European Community's move toward a unified internal market by 1992 is playing a major role in heightening interest in regional trading blocs. Some public and private sector decisionmakers are already assuming that the EC, in its implementation of the 1992 program, will discriminate against outsiders. This seems a likely possibility and something the United States should watch out for. Based on this premise, U.S. leaders are proposing remedies such as a new U.S.-Japan bilateral trade agreement or regional Pacific Rim pacts to counter any discrimination. The new agreements would be part of a special "GATT Plus" for like-minded nations.

However, these leaders have overlooked the traditional weapon that is already in place to check possible discrimination, i.e., the multilateral talks where other countries can collectively lean on the EC. The United States' focus for the time being ought to be on these talks.

Although I acknowledge the usefulness of bilateral or regional trading blocs as a negotiating strategy, we should keep this threat in the background. Now is not the time to advocate additional bilateral and regional agreements. If the United States were to form bilateral agreements with other nations, the course of international trade would change. Other countries would react to the new American initiatives. For instance, if the United States were to try to form an FTA with Japan, most of the other countries in the Pacific would be knocking on Japanese—and U.S.—doors, seeking to participate also.

An additional tactical—and practical—question is who decides, and on what basis, on the next bilateral or regional FTA candidate? Some Americans might want a U.S.-Taiwan FTA or a U.S.-Korea FTA. If the United States formed an FTA with Taiwan, how would Korea respond? If a U.S.-Australia FTA were created, how would other Pacific nations react? Resentment would clearly arise from these situations.

Multilateralism is bulky and slow. It is difficult simply to get 96 countries to sit around a table. However, at the launch of the Uruguay Round in Punta del Este, the United States should have recognized the importance of coalition formation—as, for instance, demonstrated by the Cairns Group on Agriculture and the group of 48 that fashioned the Uruguay Round working document—to prod the process. Coalition formation is critically important for the multilateral talks to succeed. But because coalitions shift from issue to issue, additional bilateral deals would rob the United States of the flexibility needed to move from coalition to coalition.

At some point, America may want to accept the EC's offer to "gang up" on Japan in a multilateral forum, a strategy the EC has been pushing for years. But America may first have to join the Japanese and gang up on Europe to ensure that it does not discriminate against the United States in implementing the 1992 program.

MULTILATERAL PROGRESS AND THE EC

My main concern about 1992 is not that it will create a fortress Europe but that the EC may be unable to liberalize externally and internally at the same time. The rules of the game are changing internally within Europe, and the focus is on breaking up the European cartels; in other words, Italian firms will have to compete with French firms and so forth. Cartels and national champions will often wind up with a great deal of excess capacity. If big competitive gains are to be realized within Europe, substantial adjustment costs, including layoffs, must occur. Some European firms will shrink or go out of business. When this happens in America, protectionist pressures increase on Capitol Hill; I would expect the same response in European parliaments.

Suppose you are an executive with a small Spanish firm. You faced new competition several years ago when you joined the European Community. Now a Europe without internal borders is planned. Your Spanish firm will have to compete more and in new ways with French and English firms. Then the Directorate of External Affairs of the EC says, "By the way, we're also going to liberalize at the border of the Community." More than likely you would throw up your hands and say, "I've had enough. No mas."

Hence, my argument is not that Europe will raise new barriers, but that it will be reluctant to lower existing ones and to liberalize under the Uruguay Round. Again, the EC may be a foot-dragger (as it has been historically) in the Uruguay Round, and America will have to put substantial pressure on the Community to keep the process open.

Although there are numerous negative consequences, there is an advantage—many of the issues being negotiated in the Uruguay Round and EC 1992 are the same. If these issues could be changed simultaneously, potential EC discrimination could be minimized. But if the EC drags its feet, the multilateral talks may lose their credibility as a means of solving problems.

Thus, the problem with EC 1992 is not merely possible discrimination—and, as noted, the United States must watch out for that. The bigger problem is that the Europeans will take their time and in the process hold the multilateral negotiations hostage to their internal restructuring. When push comes to shove—and when political will, time and resources are scarce—European attention will go to EC 1992 and not to the multilateral talks.

U.S. OPTIONS

If the multilateral negotiations stall, how will the United States react? Leaders on Capitol Hill and perhaps even in the Bush Administration may then look to regional or bilateral initiatives to make any progress.

A credible argument can be made that a bilateral, or North American, agreement with Mexico is in the long-term strategic interests of the United States for reasons that range from demographics to drugs, from debt to democracy. A bilateral or regional pact might help to obtain the objective of a sound Mexico and to maintain the credibility of the trading bloc threat.

On the other hand, there are several arguments against such a pact. There is potential opposition from Canada (as discussed), from Mexican nationalists and perhaps also from U.S. labor-intensive industries and unions. A U.S.-Mexico FTA may thus not soon become a reality. Could the United States grant preferential access to Korea or Taiwan but not to Mexico? It would be unwise to take this course of action.

The real concern is that America might give up the GATT system. Certainly in the short run, U.S. trade policy must stick with the multilateral process. If necessary, the U.S. should also "stick it" to other countries unilaterally to prod progress—the new Super 301 process is one way of doing this.

The United States must pay close attention to the U.S.-Canada FTA. If the FTA should look as though it might fail, the credibility of any bilateral threat would be undermined, and the progress of the Uruguay Round would be slowed. This would provide additional arguments to foot-draggers like the EC, who would point to the failure of even the United States and Canada, with their strong trade ties and similar business environments, to agree on new issues. American credibility would be lost, and the GATT would be damaged. Making the U.S.-Canada FTA work will be a big job, but it must be a U.S. priority. Other bilateral agreements should not be attempted for the time being.

The path that America takes in the international trade arena will influence the direction of the global economy. If the United States is seen as giving up on the GATT in favor of regional trading blocs, the GATT system will be unable to withstand the resulting pressures. The GATT needs the United States, and in the 1990s the United States will need a strong GATT in order to expand its exports and continue its economic growth.

Blocs: Making the Best of a "Second-Best" Solution

3

by Richard V.L. Cooper

The issue is not whether there ought to be regional trading blocs, for the world economy is already moving in that direction. Instead, the issue is how to maximize the benefits that regional trading blocs can create and at the same time minimize the harm they can cause in the world trading system.

A HISTORICAL PERSPECTIVE

Prior to the formation of the General Agreement on Tariffs and Trade in the late 1940s, the world trading system and indeed the world economy were limping along at best. The combination of the Great Depression, reciprocal rounds of destructive tariff increases and World War II had left the global economy stagnant and the global trading system in a state of disarray.

This situation began to change with the establishment of the GATT in 1948. The next three decades witnessed unprecedented growth in world economic prosperity, much of it brought about by a corresponding increase in world trade. Between 1950 and 1980, world trade expanded about 40-fold in nominal terms and more than 10-fold in real terms. Much of the growth in world trade, in turn, can be attributed to the GATT, not only through the specific rules it set forth, but also through the process and spirit that prompted its formation. Thus, despite the recent maligning of the effectiveness of the GATT, the GATT has helped to accomplish a great deal.

Turmoil, Dislocations and Piecemeal Protectionism

In contrast to the relative tranquility of trading relationships during the 1950s and 1960s, the trade environment since the late 1970s has been filled with turmoil. Myriad antidumping complaints, voluntary restraint agreements, fractious trade negotiations, and miniature trade wars have occurred over the past 10 years. Ironically, this turmoil in many ways was created by the GATT's enormous successes in the earlier decades. The multilateral system originally envisioned by the GATT was designed to enhance prosperity and competitiveness around the globe. Japan's rise to international prominence in the 1960s and the emergence of the Four Tigers in Asia, Brazil and Malaysia in the 1970s and 1980s are at least partially the result of the freer and more open international trading environment that the GATT fostered.

At the same time, the tremendous economic successes of Japan, Korea and the other newly industrializing economies (NIEs) during the past 10 years have had a major and sometimes adverse impact on the United States and Europe. U.S. and European markets continue to be the largest in the world, with enormous purchasing power. New entrepreneurs in Taiwan, the chaebol in Korea, major trading companies in Japan, and aircraft manufacturers in Brazil look to these markets for sales. For example, Brazilians do not expect to sell many airplanes to Argentina or Bolivia; instead, they concentrate on selling in U.S. or European markets.

These developing country strategies have, of course, created major industrial dislocations in the United States and Europe. Dislocations have occurred in automobiles, steel, photographic equipment, textiles and apparel, footware, and toys, to name just a few of many areas. Companies have gone out of business, downsized or been acquired, which in turn has resulted in the loss of many well-paying manufacturing jobs. Thus, although the world as a whole has benefited greatly from the new-found prosperity, this growth has sometimes come at a high price in terms of dislocations, particularly in the United States and Europe.

Who is responsible for our lack of response to the challenges from Japan, the NIEs and other developing countries? The realistic answer involves management, labor and government—all share in the blame.

Even though American industry is now experiencing a marked turnaround and is generally much more competitive than it was 10 years ago, problem areas still exist in many industries. European companies are not yet as competitive as much of U.S. industry, but the Europeans too are more competitive today than a decade earlier.

To date, the U.S. response to these outside pressures has largely been political, primarily in the form of piecemeal protectionism. There has been greater enforcement of antidumping laws and the imposition of new or extended voluntary restraint agreements. The continued use of VRAs troubles some analysts (including this author) because these agreements transfer wealth from U.S. consumers to foreign manufacturers. When some type of protectionism is warranted, as it sometimes is, the use of border tariffs would be more effective. With border tariffs, the wealth transfer is at least kept in the U.S.—from the American consumer to the American Treasury rather than to foreign manufacturers or governments. The Europeans have followed similar piecemeal strategies, using specialized labor laws, local content requirements and other means to protect their industries.

A PERIOD OF REGROUPING

The 1990s may also be a tumultuous period, but the underlying fundamentals should be different from those that created the turmoil of the past decade. In one sense, the 1990s will be a period of regrouping. Regional trading blocs will be an important part of this process principally because they allow countries and companies to begin to adapt to the numerous economic changes now taking place at a *more manageable* level.

In terms of the recently implemented U.S.-Canada Free Trade Agreement, for example, it is much easier for a company on either side of the St. Lawrence to attempt to be more competitive than its northern or southern industry rival than for that company to tackle the entire global system at once. The consumer electronics industry presents another example. The Europeans currently face problems similar to those that confronted the U.S. industry. The European Community's plans to form an internal market by 1992 offer Europeans a way to sustain a consumer electronics industry that may be better able to cope with the tremendous increases in competition from Japan and the other NIEs.

BENEFITS AND COSTS

The key benefit of regional trading blocs is thus their use in easing the way back to a full-blown multilateral trading system, which we currently do not have. Although the GATT provides an umbrella, it is fraught with holes. The current Uruguay Round testifies to the importance of reforming the GATT—and to the difficulty of doing so. Progress will be slow whether it is in areas involving protected markets in the developing countries or European preoccupation with EC 1992. Given these realities, regional trading blocs at least offer the opportunity to work toward the larger goal of a more open multilateral trading system in a stepwise fashion.

The dangers and costs of regional blocs, on the other hand, are obvious. Put simply, trading blocs increase the possibility of a major breakdown in the multilateral trading system. There is no doubt that this could happen if trading blocs become too inward-focused and thus end up slowing overall world trade. Much of the concern within the United States and Japan about EC 1992, for instance, revolves around worries that the reforms will slow trade between the EC and the rest of the world. History shows that slowing world trade in this fashion can have disastrous consequences for overall world prosperity.

Therefore, the key is to minimize the potential harm that these blocs can create. This means that, to the extent that regional blocs develop, they need to be kept within the rules and spirit of the GATT. This goal is possible, I believe, and has been achieved with the U.S.-Canada FTA. It can also be realized with EC 1992, but 1992 harbors some real dangers. The notion of reciprocity, for example, is a dangerous concept that could ultimately undermine not only the EC's internal market plans and European relations with outside countries, but also the multilateral trading system in general.

In addition, there are myths about perceived dangers in trading blocs. One current myth is that proposed EC 1992 domestic content regulations will create major problems for U.S. industries in that they will have to be based in Europe to conduct business there. However, the domestic content issue will probably not be a major problem with 1992 because companies in general are increasingly discovering that they have to maintain a physical presence to conduct business successfully in any major market. It is true that small companies can successfully export to, for instance, the United States, but to enter that market in a significant way, firms need to locate marketing, manufacturing and even product development there. The Japanese have taken this strategy with their automobile industry, and the Europeans have used it in other industries. The strategy has nothing to do with politics or free trade agreements; it is simply a business reality—as a company reaches a certain scale of operation, it tends to locate near its major markets. If companies are to succeed in the European market on a major scale, they will have to locate operations there regardless of the specifics of the regulations implementing EC 1992.

WHERE DO WE GO FROM HERE?

Let us briefly look at present and potential regional trading blocs around the world in an effort to determine where they fit in the context of a longer-term multilateral trading environment.

The U.S.-Canada FTA is a good model for regional trading blocs. However, Americans and Canadians should not be too self-congratulatory since the issues involved were in many ways easy to tackle given the numerous economic and cultural similarities of both countries (with the possible exception of the French-speaking areas of Canada). Many companies, in fact, already follow an integrated North American strategy. At the same time, Americans and Canadians should be proud that the FTA successfully dealt with tough issues, even though it left some areas unaddressed. Equally important, the agreement is within the spirit of the GATT.

The next real test will be in Europe. The issues there are much tougher than those the United States and Canada confronted in negotiating the FTA. The Europeans are dealing with many more countries and languages, far more different systems and much more entrenched barriers. Still, the progress to date has been remarkable. To the extent that EC 1992 is successful, it will auger well for the notion of regional trading blocs as vehicles for reentry into the larger global trading system.

Asia is more difficult to evaluate. Although some analysts believe the East Asian NIEs would rather join an FTA with the United States than with Japan, I do not think the NIEs will establish a trading bloc with the United States in any form. But it is plausible they will do so with Japan, not because of an inherent desire, but because of economic necessity. For example, Japan dominates investment flows into Malaysia, Thailand and Taiwan. This domination, combined with growing U.S. protectionism, will lead to an increase in at least informal economic alliances among some of the Asian countries, despite their very different backgrounds and heritages.

Just as the different backgrounds of the European nations have created difficulties for the EC 1992 program, so too will the far more diverse cultures of the Asian nations in any attempt to establish an FTA. Further, the Asians do not have the advantage of geographic proximity. Nevertheless, Japanese investment in East Asia is a link that will begin to tie these countries together, creating the conditions for more bloc-like behavior. Even though the East Asians will probably not set up a formal free trade zone in the sense of EC 1992, they will begin, over time, to behave more as a de facto trading bloc.

Latin America is probably the least likely to form an effective bloc and is probably the area that could most benefit from a formal regional trading agreement. The Latin Americans could use some of the trade reforms that EC 1992 is proposing, such as reduced trade barriers that will lead to a more efficient economic environment in Europe. Yet, at least in the near term (over the next 10 to 20 years), the prospect of Latin American countries overcoming the political hurdles and forming a powerful and useful regional trading bloc is highly unlikely.

We should keep in mind that bilateral agreements are not always successful policy levers. Where they presently exist, they sometimes work. Bilateral agreements have arisen from economic and geographic rationales, intents and purposes. For example, North America, at least north of the Rio Grande, can for all intents and purposes be thought of as a market; thus, the U.S.-

Canada FTA is grounded on a solid economic and geographic premise.

Eventually, it may be in the United States' long-term political and economic interests to examine establishing a formalized trading bloc agreement with Mexico. Currently, there is a stronger economic and market rationale for making the U.S.-Canada agreement work. Within Europe, there is also a strong rationale for working toward a more common economic unit.

Once we move beyond immediate geographic and economic rationales for establishing trading blocs, free trade agreements per se seem to lose purpose. This does not mean that countries cannot or should not enter into numerous bilateral trade negotiations. It will always be in the interest of the United States to be involved in bilateral negotiations on issues that are of specific concern. For instance, some analysts, including this author, for a time favored the idea of using a U.S.-Japan FTA or a U.S.-Korea FTA as a club over the Europeans regarding EC 1992. But the problem with such agreements is that we must live with them after they are signed, and it is not clear that the consequences would have been worth the price.

There will continue to be talk about a U.S.-Japan FTA. To the extent that such talks help to close genuine gaps between our countries, these discussions are worthwhile. Major bilateral trading issues exist between the United States and other countries and, as noted, it is in our interest to pursue some quite vigorously. But our efforts should not focus on establishing a system of regional trading blocs as a serious alternative to the GATT. We should work to make existing blocs run smoothly and within the spirit of the GATT. We should take advantage of the ways regional trading blocs help economies adjust to global economic changes and use these blocs as stepping stones to a stronger multilateral trading system. However, we should recognize that broad-sweeping duplications of any existing bloc will not greatly benefit us in the long run.

Regional trading blocs are only "second-best" solutions to the problems faced by the world trading system; the best solution is a major reform of the GATT. But the chances are slim of that soon becoming a reality. We should thus continue to utilize these second-best solutions and strive to make them consistent with our long-term vision of a freer multilateral trading system.

A View from Labor

4

by Mark Anderson

Most discussions on the issue of regional trading blocs, at least in the United States, are based on a principal question: what effects do regional agreements have on efforts to liberalize trade within the current GATT multilateral framework? Indeed, this question seems to be the focus of those who view any regional bloc as alarming per se and those who believe that properly constructed regional accords such as the U.S.-Canada Free Trade Agreement can speed the process of opening all markets to the free flow of goods, investment and services. This focus presupposes that further liberalization based on the post-World War II structure of the GATT is in fact desirable and that the GATT structure is and has been a multilateral system in which the benefits and costs have been equitably divided. To put it another way, this focus assumes that the recent growth of regional trading blocs represents a significant departure from historic practices.

However, examining potential changes in the trading system through the lens of these assumptions obscures the issues that are of real importance to the United States and to organized labor. Moreover, such assumptions prevent realistic appraisal—perhaps even creative development—of the types of international trading structures that could reflect the changes in economic activity that have occurred since the formation of the GATT.

For the balance of this century and into the next, increasingly contentious political and economic interests will clash over market shares. Policies focused on extending multilateralism and trade liberalization are based on outworn assumptions and will keep the United States from confronting what labor regards as the real problems of the nation. These problems center on the large and persistent U.S. current accounts deficit, the ever increasing U.S. debt and the negative impact of these American deficits on domestic production, employment and income.

REALITY VERSUS THE FREE TRADE MYTH

If the growth of regional trading blocs actually represents a basic change from the current structure of multilateralism, then perhaps it should be applauded. The so-called multilateral trading system has not exactly been kind to American workers over the past 10 years.

More likely, however, these regional developments—certainly the more publicized ones such as the U.S.-Canada Free Trade Agreement and the proposed European single market—do not in a practical sense signify much of a shift at all. Perhaps these events serve only to make more visible the fact that a multilateral system has never really existed.

To nearly all Americans, a multilateral trading system implies at least the existence of common rules, fair practices and equal treatment among countries. It also implies the equitable sharing of costs and benefits. It is useful to remind ourselves that these characteristics cannot be found in the current international system. GATT rules, even when explicit, are honored more frequently in their breach than in their practice. The GATT itself, as is well known, sanctifies huge differences between its contracting parties in their treatment of international trade. For example, while the GATT has ruled against the manner in which a relatively tiny customs user fee is imposed in the United States, Italy's regulation that limits imports of Japanese cars to 2,500 per year is allowed because that practice has been, to use GATT terminology, grandfathered.

The General System of Preferences, the European Free Trade Association and so forth have been part of the international trading landscape for a long time. Thus, the so-called free, or liberal, trade model has never been a good picture of the real world.

THE HIGH COST OF LEADERSHIP

Until fairly recently, the United States has tolerated the continuing existence of the GATT structure in the postwar period despite large differences in behavior among member countries. The United States has been willing to bear a disproportionate share of the costs of maintaining the GATT system by keeping its markets more open to trade and investment than other countries. In this way, the United States has been able to maintain some level of political and military influence over certain nations and also to encourage worldwide economic growth.

However, the international economy has changed greatly since the 1950s, and the costs of maintaining this leadership role, at least in the field of international trade, have become intolerable. The United States cannot absorb the greater relative costs of maintaining the GATT that it did in, say, the 1960s.

In what is a very different international economic order from the 1960s, the principal issue for American workers is not multilateralism or regionalism, but rather how the United States will fashion its national policy. America must promote equitable domestic economic growth and reduce the human costs of whatever economic adjustments may be necessary due to international trade. Recent shifts in American policy have been inadequate to these tasks.

A BALANCE BETWEEN GROWTH AND EQUITY

Due to the skewed nature of the current multilateral system, labor looks on the so-called new developments such as regional trading blocs with skepticism. U.S. efforts to perpetuate the current structure and to defend an "open" trading system are not a rational solution for U.S. trade problems in general or for labor problems in particular. For labor, the multilateral approach is in many cases the root of the problem, not the solution.

This focus on simple trade liberalization makes it almost impossible for America to respond creatively to a changing world economy and, indeed, it is an explicit rejection of the view that government has a positive role to play. Essentially, the United States seems determined to cede to private interests the little authority it has left over the economy. This position bodes ill for the American worker because most of the nation's trading partners share the goal of maximizing production and employment in their countries. As a result, the United States, and most directly American workers, will continue to bear a disproportionate share of the burden. In addition, the problems facing the international economy—huge U.S. trade deficits, large surpluses in other countries, and stagnation and poverty in much of the Third World—will continue to grow.

In labor's view, any useful approach to regional trading blocs, as well as to the GATT as a whole, must seek new ways to restore a balance between growth and equity. The AFL-CIO has attempted to participate constructively in the formulation of U.S. trade and investment policy by suggesting a variety of approaches the United States could pursue in the current multilateral trade negotiations that would better balance the costs and benefits of international trade.

Labor remains especially concerned over the continued use of market distorting measures by U.S. trading partners. Where these distortions disadvantage U.S. production, the United States must do more than simply seek their reduction or removal. In the GATT talks, for example, there should be a negotiated reformulation of the authority that permits trade action for balance of payments problems. A properly constructed new authority could allow countries to take direct trade action on the problem of either a large deficit or a large surplus. Perhaps in this way some semblance of balance, now so clearly absent, could begin to be restored to the international trading system.

Trading Blocs and Human Resources— The New Wild Cards

5

by Richard S. Belous

In response to the growth of regional trading blocs and the globalization of the economy, many senior business executives have discovered that human resource policies are strategic levers that can improve the competitive advantage of their companies. In fact, in numerous cases, human resource policy changes have proven to be the key short-run strategic lever. These policies include compensation and benefit levels, employment totals, training and development, and the use of contingent workers.

REGIONAL HUMAN RESOURCE PLANNING

In the short run, corporations are often locked into certain types of technologies or capital stock and face many fixed costs that cannot be altered. However, as economists have pointed out for many years, labor is a variable cost. Thus, in the short run, the management of a multinational corporation frequently has far greater ability to adjust labor costs than other expenses.[1]

Because of these realities, American executives at a growing number of multinational corporations are starting to plan and manage human resources from a regional and/or global perspective. For example, a local division often has the choice of using a combination of American expatriates, local nationals and third country nationals in multinational staffing. A product may be designed by a subsidiary in one country and produced by a different subsidiary in another country. A division in one country may, in effect, work as a subcontractor for a different division in another country.

Due to this shift to regional and/or global planning in human resource options, some experts suggest that the term *multinational* no longer describes these corporations and that *transnational* be used instead. Whereas a multinational corporation is a group of individual national companies that are linked in a general corporate structure, a transnational corporation is a more unified economic unit that thinks and functions on regional and/or global terms. A multinational corporation is similar to a track and field team whose players generally compete in different individual events. A transnational corporation resembles a football team whose players all have to coordinate their actions for the same plays. A key feature of the transnational corporation is its blend of centralization and decentralization, and its hallmark is flexibility.[2]

Flexibility is often presented as an unmixed blessing. But if it is not humanely instituted, flexibility is far from being a net benefit for a society. In fact, one's view on flexibility may well depend upon whether one is the "flexee" or the "flexor."

Certainly labor leaders see cause for concern, as executives of major corporations have increasingly begun to think of human resource management in regional or global terms. Moreover, the creation of regional trading blocs—which result in the freer movement of goods, services and capital within the blocs—presents corporate management with even further options on the human resource front. Consider the European Community and its plans for a unified internal market by 1992. A European firm will be able to shift more of its work to those European markets that have lower labor costs. A firm will be able to expand plants in European nations with weak labor, occupational safety and health laws and to close plants in European nations with weak regulations on worker displacement.

IMPACTS ON LABOR-MANAGEMENT RELATIONS

Management's New Possibilities

The expanded transnational possibilities now open to management in the human resource area are the new wild cards in labor-management relations. Although the potential unemployment/employment aspects of regional trading blocs are frequently of concern, many econometric models show only small unemployment/employment changes resulting from the formation of a new bloc. The major human resource-related impacts resulting from creation of a bloc may affect the climate of labor-management relations more than they affect net employment totals.

For example, while the formation of a regional trading bloc may not result in massive unemployment, it could change management's outlook toward unionization. It could increase management's efforts to resist unions and establish nonunion corporate divisions. It could heighten management's desire to keep a plant, office or store open for business despite a strike by union workers. It could also create downward pressures on compensation and benefit levels. This does not mean that a corporation will always reduce the wages and benefits of its current workers. However, the corporation may increase its use of contingent workers (part-time, temporary and subcontracted labor) and institute so-called two-tiered wage and benefit systems.

Some experts have pointed out that management does not need a new regional trading bloc to create new policies such as two-tiered systems or nonunion divisions. Although this may be true, the introduction of a regional trading bloc may increase the pace of such changes.[3]

It has been argued that the changes in labor markets and corporate human resource systems discussed above may provide many benefits for a mature industrial economy. The increased labor market flexibility that has recently been established in many of these economies may help restore international competitiveness within them. If so and if the increased competitiveness results in improved productivity levels, then workers in these economies will wind up with higher compensation levels in the long run due to the creation of regional trading blocs. Furthermore, while some blue-collar jobs may be eliminated, the number of white-collar and so-called knowledge-based jobs may increase. Thus, it is argued, regional trading blocs could expand job opportunities in the long run.[4]

Labor's Responses

Labor has responded to these trade-induced changes in the climate of labor-management relations. If a regional trading bloc is created that promotes freer exchange within product markets, then the social policy area must not be forgotten, labor has insisted. In essence, labor has said that if workers now live in a global economy, we must have global labor standards.

In the case of EC 1992, it is ironic that the British Labour party has become the "party for Europe" and the British Conservative party, the "little Englander party." British Prime Minister Margaret Thatcher is calling for "slow going" on EC 1992, while European Commission officials are asking British Labour party members to "go fast."[5]

Prime Minister Thatcher's concern is that many of her labor-management victories in the United Kingdom might be reversed by the policies of a new, united Europe. Policy changes that British labor has been unable to win on the picket line or in Parliament it now hopes to win through the creation of unified labor and social policy standards for the entire European Community.[6]

American labor's response to regional and global trade has been to become more involved in U.S. trade legislation. Unfair labor practices have been tied with American trade laws that look at why various foreign producers may have a comparative advantage over the United States in certain product areas. Also, there has been a renewed effort on the part of American labor to have the United States approve various labor-related codes drafted by the International Labour Organization.

American labor leaders are concerned about the prospects of a new free trade agreement with Mexico. Such an agreement could have a major impact on U.S. labor markets.

THE IMPACTS OF THE U.S.-CANADA FTA

The U.S.-Canada FTA is a good case study of how regional trading blocs and their potential for increasing flexibility in the human resource area could be the new wild cards in labor-management relations. Although the shifts created by the FTA in the world of work have often been ignored or downplayed, they will significantly influence business, labor and public decisionmakers and have a major impact on labor-management relations in both countries.

In the long run, the result of the FTA for U.S. and Canadian workers could be a greater ability to compete in global markets. However, the net short-run result could be increased U.S. and Canadian labor market turbulence. Although the actual number of job dislocations may not be very large in terms of the aggregate U.S. and Canadian economies, pressures will be placed on various labor-management relationships. How constructively labor and management deal with these new pressures will affect the competitive climate in the two countries.

The U.S. and Canadian Industrial Relations Systems

It is no secret that many union leaders and members in the United States currently believe that the American industrial relations system is unfair to workers and that the National Labor Relations Board is stacked against labor. Beyond the specific NLRB decisions made in the conservative era of the 1980s, U.S. union leaders and workers charge that the existing NLRB system works against labor's interests in areas such as union organizing, elections, obtaining a first contract, and unfair labor practices. The answer often given to the obvious question "what should be done about it?" is "look at Canada."

The Canadian industrial relations system is sometimes referred to as the "jewel of the north" by American labor. As Table 5.1 shows, Canadian unionization rates were lower than U.S. levels in the early 1950s, but are currently much higher. Even though the Canadian rates have modestly declined in recent years, 37.6 percent of the Canadian nonfarm workforce was in the union rank and file in 1987 compared to 17 percent of the U.S. nonfarm workforce.

TABLE 5.1

U.S. AND CANADIAN UNION MEMBERSHIP AS A PERCENTAGE OF THE NONFARM WORKFORCE OF EACH COUNTRY

	U.S.	Canada
1952	33.0	21.0
1960	28.6	32.3
1970	29.6	33.6
1975	28.9	36.9
1980	23.2	37.6
1981	22.6	37.4
1982	21.9	39.0
1983	20.7	40.0
1984	19.4	39.6
1985	18.0	39.0
1986	17.5	37.7
1987	17.0	37.6

Sources: U.S. Bureau of Labor Statistics and Canadian Ministry of Labour.

What causes this vast difference in unionization levels? Canada and the United States have not differed greatly in terms of recent shifts from goods production to service production. The two countries also have many similar cultural roots and values. Some experts have identified public policy as the key factor explaining the two countries' diverse unionization rates. In the view of Harvard's Richard Freeman and James Medoff:

> The principal difference between unionization in the United States and Canada is that U.S. laws allow management to conduct lengthy, well-funded election campaigns against unions. Canada labor laws do not permit such activity. Indeed, in most provinces a union is certified without any secret ballot campaign at all: it requires only that 60 or so percent of the workers sign authorization cards. The result is growing private-sector unionization in Canada.[7]

In addition, some Canadian provinces will help a new union bargaining unit win a first contract from an employer. In the United States, it is quite possible to win a union election and then fail to obtain a first contract. In general, the Canadian labor relations system appears to be much more supportive of collective bargaining than the U.S. system. If the U.S. industrial relations system were based on the Canadian model, American unionization rates might be at least 25 percent of the workforce instead of their current 17 percent level.

Thus, there are aspects of the Canadian industrial relations system that some U.S. labor leaders and workers wish to emulate. This could be accomplished either through labor law reform in the United States or by circumventing the NLRB with a type of "off-the-books" system. A growing number of American labor experts have raised the possibility of unions representing workers de facto, i.e., bypassing the formal NLRB machinery. Both in labor law reform and in an off-the-books system, U.S. labor would use many features of the Canadian industrial relations system as a model.

However, instead of the U.S. industrial relations system moving more in the direction of the Canadian system, the Canadian system will move more toward that of the United States. A primary force behind this shift will be the FTA.

Pressures from the FTA

The FTA will create numerous pressures on the Canadian industrial relations system. As this happens, some of the Canadian model's luster could be diminished in the eyes of American labor. As shown in Table 5.2, the types of jobs generated by the Canadian and U.S. economies have been somewhat different in the 1980s. In public and social services, Canada has experienced a 20 percent job growth, whereas the United States has seen only a 14.3 percent increase. As the FTA increases economic links

TABLE 5.2

JOB GROWTH IN THE UNITED STATES AND CANADA (Percentage Change, 1980-87)

	U.S.	Canada
Total	+13.2	+11.8
Goods production	+ 0.2	− 0.5
Public and social services	+14.3	+20.0
Business and financial services	+28.3	+16.0
Consumer and personal services	+17.9	+18.3

Sources: U.S. Bureau of Labor Statistics and Statistics Canada.

between the two nations, it will be more difficult for Canada to continue to expand employment in this service sector at a much faster rate than the United States.

Evidence shows that contiguous American states can hold a sales tax gap of up to, say, 5 percentage points without the tax leakage being unbearable.[8] As with the so-called natural rate of unemployment, it might be difficult to find an exact number that represents the tax gap that is sustainable between the two countries. Even if that difficulty is overcome, the FTA represents a real constraint on Canadian public and social service employment. When Canadian collective bargaining produces conditions that are vastly different from U.S. conditions, the FTA will set in motion economic forces that will exert pressures on the unions.

Table 5.2 also indicates that job growth in business and financial services has been stronger in the United States than in Canada. Although actual unionization levels in manufacturing are very similar in the two countries, these levels are quite different in services. For example, in 1985, 33.6 percent of Canadians employed in services were unionized, but only 6.6 percent of U.S. service workers were unionized.[9] As trade in services expands under the FTA, many unionized Canadian firms will be forced to compete with nonunionized American companies.

The U.S. response to increased competition has been the rise of the nonunion industrial relations system, as MIT's Thomas Kochan and Robert McKersie and Cornell's Harry Katz note:

> When competition increases, the initial decision a firm must make is whether to remain active in that line of business and compete in the new environment or withdraw and reallocate its capital resources to other opportunities. If the firm decides to remain in the market, the next decision it must make is whether to compete on the basis of low prices (costs) and high volume or to seek out more specialized market niches that will support a price premium.
>
> The central industrial relations effect of increased sensitivity to prices and costs is that firms shift their priorities away from maintaining labor peace to controlling labor costs, streamlining work rules (so as to increase . . . efficiency), and promoting productivity. The pressure to control or lower costs is especially intense if a firm attempts to compete . . . on the basis of low prices and high volume.[10]

One of the major reasons cited for Canadian interest in the FTA is that it will help Canadian firms increase their economies of scale due to higher volume. But if Canadian producers are able to increase volume and lower prices, their central industrial relations priority will shift from maintaining labor peace to controlling labor costs. In some cases, this shift in priority has already taken place, and it has not waited for the FTA.

Relative Labor Costs

The FTA will increase competition between American and Canadian workers, and relative labor costs will play a key role. How do Canadian labor costs compare with U.S. levels? A recent Conference Board of Canada study noted that in 1966 Canadian earnings were higher than those in the United States in only 2 out of 63 industries studied on an exchange rate-adjusted basis. However, by 1976, a rapid buildup of Canadian wages resulted in 54 out of 63 Canadian industries exceeding U.S. levels. Yet, in 1986 only 13 out of 63 Canadian industries were above the U.S. level.[11] These data seem to indicate that Canadian labor costs have been fairly competitive with U.S. levels. However, as indicated in Table 5.3, additional factors must be considered. For example, Canadian manufacturing earnings increased from 85 percent of the U.S. level in 1980 to 89 percent in 1987; these earnings were still much greater than the relative levels of, say, 1966 (76 percent). In the major industry groups examined, Canadian earnings averaged 20 percent below U.S. levels in 1966, but only 10 percent below in 1986.[12] At the same time, Canadian earnings in finance, insurance and real estate were still above U.S. levels, and in services they were about the same.

TABLE 5.3

CANADIAN EARNINGS AS A PERCENTAGE OF U.S. EARNINGS BY MAJOR INDUSTRIAL GROUPS, 1966-87

	1966	1976	1980	1986	1987
Manufacturing	76	111	85	88	89
Transportation	75	102	na	88	na
Wholesale	80	119	na	87	na
Retail	91	137	na	109	na
Finance, insurance and real estate	93	140	na	106	na
Services	85	112	na	99	na
Construction	67	116	na	80	na
Mining	80	117	na	91	na

na = not available.
Sources: The Conference Board of Canada and the U.S. Bureau of Labor Statistics.

The data presented in Table 5.4 point to additional concerns for Canadian labor and management. Since 1979, U.S. productivity growth (3.4 percent per year, on average) has been much higher than Canadian productivity growth (2.2 percent per year, on average). Also since 1979, U.S. unit labor costs (2.2 percent per year, on average) have been increasing at a much lower rate than Canadian unit labor costs (5.2 percent per year, on average). Thus, in recent years, Canada has experienced lower productivity growth than the United States. At the same time, Canada's earnings growth has been higher than that of the United States in terms of own-country currency. The depreciation of the Canadian dollar has been the primary factor keeping Canadian labor costs lower than U.S. costs.

In general, a nation can maintain competitive labor costs relative to its trading partners by two means: a shift in exchange rates, and changes in its labor markets, including wage adjustments and/or various institutional changes. In recent years, Canada has most often used exchange rate shifts to keep its labor costs competitive.

For example, as noted above, actual Canadian manufacturing earnings increased from 85 percent of the U.S. level in 1980 to 89 percent in 1987. If U.S.-Canadian exchange rates had remained fixed in this period, Canadian manufacturing earnings in

TABLE 5.4

U.S. AND CANADIAN MANUFACTURING PRODUCTIVITY AND UNIT LABOR COST TRENDS (Average Annual Growth Rates)

	Productivity	
	U.S.	**Canada**
1970-75	2.8%	3.2%
1975-80	1.7	2.0
1979-87	3.4	2.2
	Unit Labor Costs	
	U.S.	**Canada**
1970-75	4.9%	7.1%
1975-80	10.3	8.6
1979-87	2.2	5.2

Sources: The Conference Board of Canada and the U.S. Bureau of Labor Statistics.

1987 might have been higher than such earnings in the United States (see Table 5.5). Thus, a falling value of the Canadian dollar has been the main factor that has kept Canadian labor costs competitive. As the Conference Board of Canada has concluded:

> Given current productivity levels, increased competition brought about by freer trade will mean further pressure to moderate increases in Canadian earnings. This should result in less dependence upon the value of the Canadian dollar in maintaining a competitive advantage.[13]

At the start of the 1990s, the value of the Canadian dollar was increasing compared to the value of the U.S. dollar. This was due to the tight monetary policies of the Bank of Canada. While tight Canadian money can bring down inflation in Canada, it can also make Canadian exports and labor less competitive with U.S. exports and labor.

What does this growing wave of pressures on the Canadian industrial relations system mean for labor markets? The FTA will create more of a "general equilibrium" system, to use the language of economists. This system—which links many markets together—is noted for its "spillover" and "feedback" effects. The initial jolt of the FTA could be a spillover effect in which the U.S. indus-

TABLE 5.5

ACTUAL CANADIAN MANUFACTURING EARNINGS AND ESTIMATED EARNINGS IF THE FOREIGN EXCHANGE RATE HAD REMAINED FIXED (As a Percentage of U.S. Earnings)

	1980	1987
Actual manufacturing earnings	85	89
Estimated manufacturing earnings if exchange rates had remained fixed*	85	101

*Canadian earnings as a percentage of U.S. earnings based on 1980 foreign exchange rates.

Note: The estimates presented here are based on partial equilibrium. A fuller treatment would be based on a general equilibrium model in which the impact of a fixed exchange rate would be felt on all parts of the system.

Source: Author's estimates based on U.S. Bureau of Labor Statistics data.

trial relations system will influence the Canadian model. But if Canadian labor and management learn how to reduce their costs and boost productivity relative to the United States, there will be a feedback effect on U.S. labor markets. American labor and management could be forced to make new labor market adjustments to counter improved Canadian competition.

Capital Flows and Labor

Capital flows could figure prominently in FTA impacts on labor in both countries. Some experts have pointed to hopes for increased injections of capital into Canada as a major reason behind the Canadian support of the FTA.[14] If this happens, the Canadian capital-labor ratio would rise. All other factors being equal, many economists would then expect the value of average real wages in Canada also to increase.

However, in recent years, Canada has experienced a negative net flow of capital (see Table 5.6).[15] Can the FTA reverse this trend? It can be argued that if Canadian producers obtain more reliable shares of U.S. markets, investment in Canadian production facilities will increase, which could reverse the trend.

This argument is based on several big "ifs." First, it is predicated on Canadian producers winding up with larger North Ameri-

TABLE 5.6

ANNUAL DIRECT INVESTMENT FLOWS INVOLVING CANADA, 1960-87 (Mill. Can. $)

	Foreign Direct Investment in Canada	Canadian Direct Investment Abroad	Net Flows
1960-64	+ 457	– 93	+ 364
1965-69	+ 665	– 170	+ 495
1970-74	+ 825	– 505	+ 322
1975-79	+ 357	–1,424	–1,067
1980-84	– 540	–3,530	–4,070
1985	–2,950	–5,100	–7,850
1986	+1,550	–4,521	–2,971
1987	+4,361	–6,009	–1,648

Sources: Alan M. Rugman, *Outward Bound: Canadian Direct Investment in the United States* (Washington, D.C. and Toronto, Ont.: Canadian-American Committee, 1987); and Statistics Canada.

can market shares than they currently have. This might not happen. Further, it assumes the FTA will set in motion a process that will minimize various forms of so-called contingent protection (e.g., antidumping, countervailing duties and escape clause actions). This, of course, remains to be seen. Finally, the argument assumes that all other factors will remain equal. In the next few years, domestic U.S. macroeconomic considerations may swamp the capital flow implications of the FTA. If U.S. monetary policy remains tight—and results in high U.S. interest rates—the net capital outflows from Canada could persist.

In summary, the FTA will place some strains on the industrial relations systems in Canada and the United States. In Canada, a floating exchange rate will more than ever before require labor market safety valves in the form of wage adjustments and institutional changes if labor costs are to remain competitive. As the Canadian system adjusts to the resulting pressures, new competitive forces will arise to help restrain American labor costs.

In the long run, the net result of the FTA may be to increase the ability of U.S. and Canadian production facilities to compete in international markets. In the short run, however, U.S. and Canadian labor markets could be faced with increased pressures.

REGIONAL TRADING BLOCS AND LABOR MOBILITY

Blocs could also have a significant impact on labor mobility. Although Adam Smith wrote *The Wealth of Nations* long before the United States and Canada signed a free trade agreement and the European Community began plans for an integrated market, his observations could accurately describe the net impacts of free trade agreements on labor mobility. Smith noted the key links between various product, capital and labor markets; as the "free circulation" of one factor of production is increased, there will be increased pressures for greater circulation of the other factors of production. Or, as Smith put it, "whatever obstructs the free circulation of labor from one employment to another, obstructs that of stock likewise."[16]

The U.S.-Canada Free Trade Agreement does not directly address international labor market mobility. However, the European plans to form an internal market by 1992 include various provisions to increase the ability of workers in one EC nation to obtain work in another. For example, the plans provide for the recognition of academic degrees and other training qualifications between Community countries.[17]

International labor mobility thus becomes the focus of key policy questions. For instance, as the number of corporations expands in various regional and international product and capital markets, will labor markets become more regional and international? Will agreements like EC 1992 and the FTA increase the flow of labor across borders?

NPA Survey Results

In an effort to further our understanding of the potential impacts of free trade agreements on labor markets, the National Planning Association recently surveyed the U.S. members of its committees. These 480 top corporate executives, labor leaders, professionals, and noted academics were polled on their expectations regarding labor-related trade issues. Many of NPA's committee members have developed strategies for dealing with these issues within their own organizations.

On the issue of labor mobility, 68 percent of the executives who responded to the survey believe that the U.S.-Canada FTA will increase the mobility of white-collar workers over the border. However, 57 percent expect that the agreement will not increase the mobility of blue-collar workers between the two countries (see Chart 5.1).

In terms of Europe 1992, 79 percent of the executives expect that the mobility of white-collar workers across European Community borders will increase; 59 percent believe that EC 1992 will also result in increased blue-collar mobility (see Chart 5.2).

Based on these expectations, then, the following should occur:

- as free trade agreements increase the international flow of products, the international flow of labor will also increase; and
- free trade agreements will have a stronger impact on white-collar than on blue-collar international labor mobility.

The NPA survey results also indicate that the views of management and labor can differ on the prospects of expanding international labor mobility. Management respondents generally expect the added labor flow to generate many benefits, including:

- increased opportunities for multinational corporations to develop multinational human resource strategies;
- a growing supply of talented and flexible workers; and
- a potential for reduced labor costs.

Labor respondents, however, foresee problems from the increased labor flow over borders. These include:

- downward pressure on wages and employee benefits; and
- pressure on nations that provide more liberal social welfare programs to reduce benefit levels.

CHART 5.1

Will the Impact of the U.S.-Canadian Free Trade Agreement Increase the Mobility of Workers Across the Border?

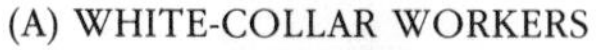

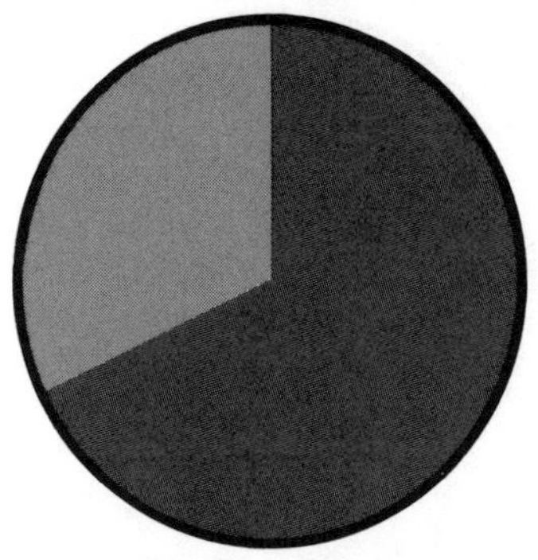

32% NO, there will not be increased mobility.

68% YES, there will be increased mobility.

(B) BLUE-COLLAR WORKERS

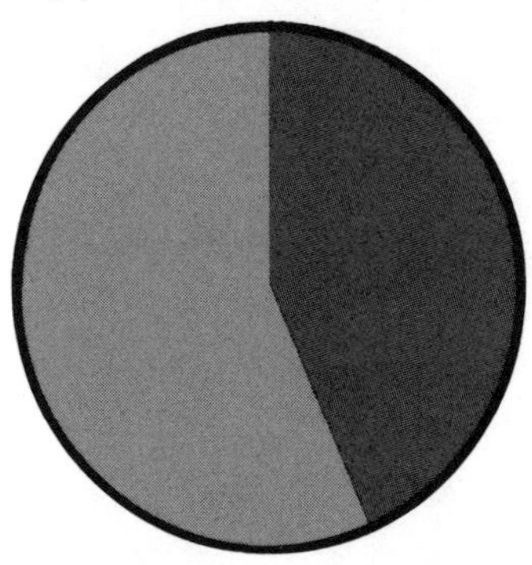

57% NO, there will not be increased mobility.

43% YES, there will be increased mobility.

Source: NPA Survey of International Committee-Member Executives.

As one union leader noted in response to the NPA survey:

> Our union is not eager to encourage increased cross-border mobility by workers when unemployment and underemployment are important problems with no resolution in sight. Differences in national unemployment compensation systems and other social programs may put countries with higher standards at a disadvantage. Increased international competition

CHART 5.2

Will the Impact of EC Plans to Form a Unified Internal Market by 1992 Increase the Mobility of Workers Across European Borders?

(A) WHITE-COLLAR WORKERS

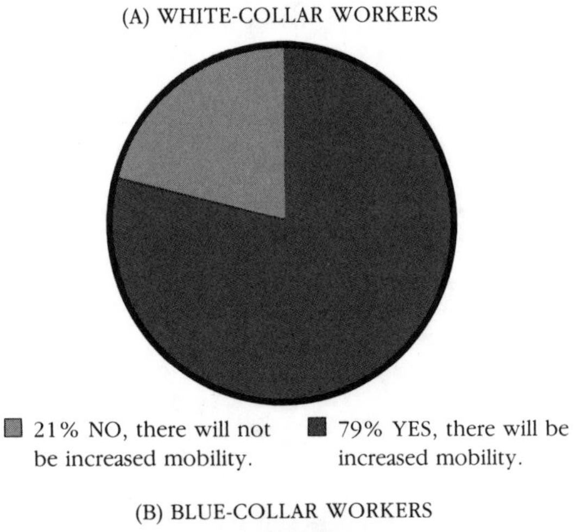

(B) BLUE-COLLAR WORKERS

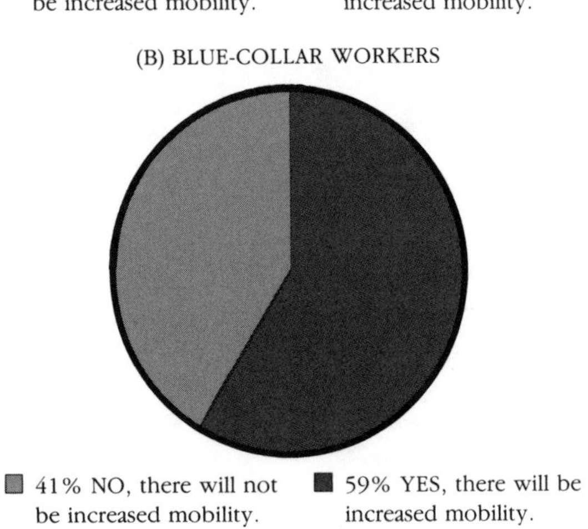

Source: NPA Survey of International Committee-Member Executives.

for scarce jobs is not a solution . . . unions in general would endorse; it will only lead to lower compensation and weaker labor standards.

POLICY IMPLICATIONS

Public decisionmakers have given little thought to the implications of increased international labor mobility caused by free trade agreements, with a few exceptions. The Canadian Council on Professional Engineers and the Canadian Bar Association have established committees to deal with issues resulting from FTA-generated growth in cross-border traffic, and some Canadian experts have expressed concern that the expanded cross-border movement of executives and professionals could result in a Canadian "brain drain" similar to that of the 1960s.[18]

One way to further our understanding of international labor mobility is to measure it. But the United States and many other countries do not compile data on this subject. For instance, statistics on the numbers of Canadians currently working in the United States (or on the number of U.S. citizens working in Canada) are not available in the United States. According to the Immigration and Naturalization Service, the Bureau of Labor Statistics and the Census Bureau, the U.S. government does not publish statistics in this area.

Canadian statistics are only somewhat better. By using data from Statistics Canada, NPA was able to determine that 3.4 percent of the Canadian labor force was employed in the United States in 1981. Estimates beyond 1981 could not be produced.

Many changes have taken place in the economy since the American labor force data system was established at the end of the Great Depression. The "closed" U.S. economy of that time is now much more "open" to international forces, yet the U.S. labor force data system generally has not been adjusted to reflect the new realities. A key policy change should be to redirect this data system to deal with international labor flows. Business and labor may sometimes disagree on whether increased international labor flows are "good" or "bad" for society. But public decisionmakers, corporate executives and labor leaders must be able to measure international labor mobility if they are to fashion sound economic and trade policies.

As MIT's Paul Krugman and the University of Pennsylvania's Maurice Obstfeld have noted:

> Although there is fundamental economic similarity between trade and factor movements . . . there are major differences in the political context. . . . A capital-abundant country may import labor-intensive goods or begin employing migrant workers. . . . On the whole, international factor movement tends to raise even more political difficulties than international trade.[19]

In addition to the FTA and Europe 1992, potential free trade agreements between the United States and Mexico and between the United States and various newly industrializing countries are being seriously discussed. The consequences of such free trade agreements cannot be ignored by public decisionmakers and analysts, as the NPA survey and other evidence show.

It is understandable that the product market impacts of regional trading blocs have been examined more thoroughly than their labor market and social policy impacts. But recent trends in international trade will have a major influence on labor-management relations. It does not appear possible to go back to an era of mostly national product and capital markets. The growth of regional trading blocs has already produced serious jolts to traditional corporate human resource systems.

NOTES

1. Richard S. Belous, *The Contingent Economy: The Growth of the Temporary, Part-Time and Subcontracted Workforce* (Washington, D.C.: National Planning Association, 1989), pp. 2-6.
2. *The Financial Times*, July 6, 1989, p. 14.
3. This observation is based on the comments of several American and Canadian economists on this chapter.
4. For more on these types of arguments, see Richard S. Belous and Andrew W. Wyckoff, "Trade Has Job Winners Too," *Across the Board* (September 1987), pp. 58-61.
5. *The Economist*, July 8, 1989, pp. 42-48.
6. Hugo Young, *One of Us: A Biography of Margaret Thatcher* (London: MacMillan, 1989), pp. 143, 190-191, 381-388.
7. Richard B. Freeman and James L. Medoff, *What Do Unions Do?* (New York: Basic Books, 1984), p. 242.
8. *The Economist*, July 9, 1988, pp. 8-15.
9. Data for 1985 are from the Canadian Ministry of Labour and the U.S. Bureau of Labor Statistics.
10. Thomas A. Kochan, Harry C. Katz and Robert B. McKersie, *The Transformation of American Industrial Relations* (New York: Basic Books, 1986), p. 65.
11. Sperry Lea, "A Historical Perspective," in *Perspectives on a U.S.-Canadian Free Trade Agreement*, ed. Robert M. Stern et al. (Washington, D.C. and Ottawa, Ont.: Brookings Institution and Institute for Research on Public Policy, 1987), pp. 11-29.
12. Judith Lendvay-Zwickl, *How Well Do We Compete? Relative Labour Costs in Canada and the United States* (Ottawa, Ont.: Conference Board of Canada, 1988), pp. 1-4.
13. Ibid., p. vi.
14. Ibid.
15. Lea, "Historical Perspective," pp. 23-28.
16. Adam Smith, *The Wealth of Nations* (New York: Modern Library, 1965), pp. 134-135.
17. Michael Calingaert, *The 1992 Challenge from Europe: Development of the European Community's Internal Market* (Washington, D.C.: National Planning Association, 1988), pp. 22-23, 66-69.
18. *The Financial Post*, January 2, 1989, p. 7.
19. Paul R. Krugman and Maurice Obstfeld, *International Economics: Theory and Policy* (Glenview, Ill.: Scott, Foresman and Company, 1988), p. 149.

America's Role in the Founding of the European Community

6

by Herbert E. Weiner

The central role of the United States in the 1948 founding of the General Agreement on Tariffs and Trade is well-known. For the United States, this participation was part of a dedicated effort after World War II to create a liberalized world trading system and preempt a return to the ruinous protective trade practices of the interwar years.

These actions also fit the key role the United States assumed in the formation of a major regional trading bloc, the European Community. Although current European plans to form a unified internal market by 1992 are of concern to some Americans, we should be reminded that in many ways the creation of the EC stemmed from a shared and profound belief in a partnership between a united Europe and the United States. Such cooperation would not have been possible with a fragmented Europe. More important, European unity was seen as essential to carrying the banner of freedom, equality and democracy throughout the globe.

The United States, via the Marshall Plan in the late 1940s, strongly supported "those efforts of certain innovative leaders in France, Germany, Italy, and the Low Countries to form a customs union that would be the first step toward an eventual" unified EC. "For Western Europe, the revolutionary goal of U.S. policy was the replacement of the region's system of independent nation-states by a political and economic union capable of defending itself and of helping to maintain the integration, security, and orderliness of the international system."[1]

Thus, U.S. activities in the international trading field have been at several different levels. While the United States has been a major champion of multilateralism, at the same time it has fostered the growth of a significant regional trading bloc within the multilateral system.

POSTWAR CRISIS

American policy toward Europe in the late 1940s was forged as a pragmatic response to a mounting economic and political crisis. The vast destruction of European production capacity was threatening a collapse of social order in much of Europe. Shortages of food and fuel (particularly coal, Europe's overwhelming source of energy) were becoming severe, with adverse chain reactions in the workforce and in the production of goods needed for reconstruction, e.g., steel and machinery. Inflation was accelerating, and governments, having used much of their income-producing foreign assets and reserves to pay for the war, were becoming desperately short of foreign exchange as U.S. loans and grants ran out. It has been estimated that between 1938 and 1947, on the average, the European standard of living (i.e., per capita gross national product in constant dollars) fell by more than 8 percent. In Italy, the decline exceeded 25 percent; in West Germany, more than 15 percent; in France, nearly 10 percent; in the Low Countries, 6 to 7 percent; and in Austria and Greece, almost 40 percent. By contrast, per capita GNP had increased about 4 percent in the United Kingdom and almost 50 percent in the United States.[2]

However, these statistics do not begin to capture the total devastating impact of the war on the European social and political fabric of the late 1940s. It was a bad situation that Americans had every reason to expect would worsen in the absence of a bold and visionary plan to put the European nations on a self-supporting basis. The Soviet Union, on the other hand, saw opportunities to extend Soviet hegemony and proceeded aggressively to capitalize politically on the destruction wrought by World War II. The United States thus could not afford to retreat into isolation as it had done after World War I.

In addition, key American government, business and labor leaders realized in the late 1940s that the United States would face serious problems in the long run if Europe did not get back on its economic feet. An exhausted Europe, lacking financial and productive capital, could not be a growing trading partner with the United States. Even though America might have financial and real capital, the country also needed healthy trading relationships with European nations. It was therefore in America's interest to promote a revitalized Europe.

THE MARSHALL PLAN AND THE ECA

It was in this context that the Marshall Plan played a vital role in the formation of the European Community. The Plan not only provided the needed capital to prime the European pump, but also seeded the process of creating a unified European economy. The EC credits the strategic and "visionary" role that the Marshall Plan played in the enormous revival of EC-U.S. trade (more than 30 percent of the world total by 1986) and of mutual capital investment.[3]

To address the severe problems noted above, George C. Marshall—with the strong support of President Truman and after internal study by the Department of State—presented the general outline of what became known as the Marshall Plan at Harvard's commencement on June 5, 1947.

The Truman Administration had done its homework to make the Marshall Plan bipartisan, winning a wide range of support from Republicans and Democrats, business and labor. The support of Republican Senator Arthur H. Vandenberg of Michigan was crucial. Vandenberg was the chairman of the Senate Foreign Relations Committee. He had also been a leader of conservative isolationist forces before the war. However, new realities convinced Vandenberg that the Marshall Plan—and active American involvement overseas—was required in the postwar world.

Vandenberg had a significant influence on the shape and direction of the Marshall Plan. He convinced the Truman Administration that the Plan should be directed by business and other private sector leaders rather than operated by "government types" directly out of the State Department. As a result, the independent Economic Cooperation Administration was established to administer the program, with Paul C. Hoffman, president of the Studebaker Corporation (a Republican and Vandenberg's candidate), nominated by President Truman to head the ECA.

The Marshall Plan provided $13.3 billion in assistance to Europe from 1948 to 1952. In 1988 dollars, this total is equal to approximately $53 billion. In fiscal 1948, roughly 11 cents out of every federal dollar was used to fund the Marshall Plan. Currently, only about 2 cents out of every federal dollar is used to support the entire U.S. foreign affairs budget. Thus, the Marshall Plan was a large undertaking even by today's standards.

The ECA extended into many other areas besides providing grants and fostering investment. It had a very active technical assistance program, which introduced many American management and production practices to European businesses. It promoted "people to people" diplomacy. It encouraged the formation of free and independent trade unions as an institutional bulwark for democracy and labor-management cooperation to spur productivity and distribute its fruits for the benefit of all.

THE EUROPEAN DREAM

A few weeks after Marshall's Harvard speech, British Foreign Secretary Ernest Bevin and French Foreign Minister Georges Bidault issued a joint communique inviting 22 European nations to send representatives to Paris to formulate a cooperative recovery plan. Sixteen accepted, convening in Paris in July 1948. They

ALLOCATION OF ASSISTANCE PROVIDED UNDER THE MARSHALL PLAN, 1948–52
(Mill. 1948 U.S. $)

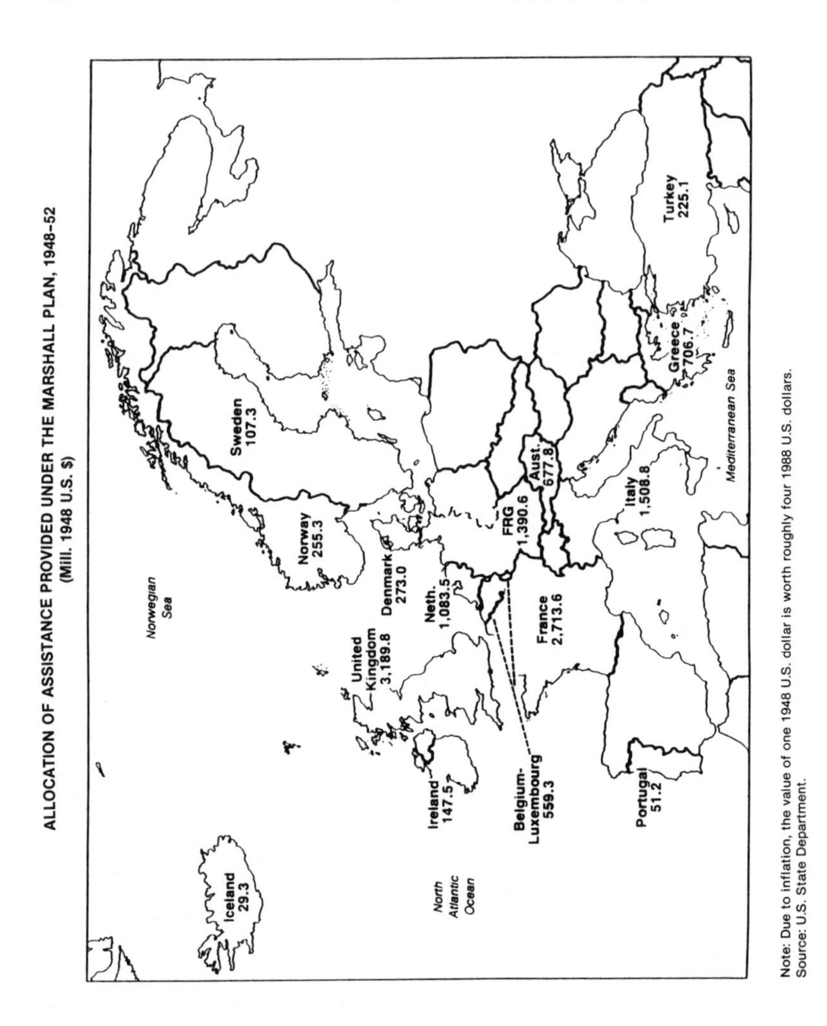

Note: Due to inflation, the value of one 1948 U.S. dollar is worth roughly four 1988 U.S. dollars.
Source: U.S. State Department.

formed the Organization for European Economic Cooperation. (The OEEC in a broad sense led to the founding in 1961 of the Organization for Economic Cooperation and Development to stimulate economic development and world trade.) Poland, Yugoslavia and Czechoslovakia were pressured by Moscow to stay out of the Paris meetings—and the Marshall Plan. The Soviet Union instead made the Marshall Plan the focus of its attack during the Cold War.

The ECA encouraged European government, business and labor leaders to think in European terms and in terms of cooperative planning. American and European concerns were not only economic; the direction of Germany after the war was a major issue. A revitalized Germany, it was hoped, could be linked in economic cooperation with France and other European nations, putting an end to an old source of war. The imaginative proposal in May 1950 by French Foreign Minister Robert Schuman and that grand pragmatic "citizen of Europe" Jean Monnet to establish a European Coal and Steel Community ("The Six") stemmed from the shared goal, nourished by American efforts, of realizing the vision of Europe-wide cooperation. The establishment of the ECSC also was a basic step in efforts to weave West Germany and France into a system of peaceful economic relations. The ECSC was a first stage from which came the treaty creating the European Economic Community (and the European Atomic Energy Community) in 1957. While it may seem many years between the 1951 treaty and the plans to form a unified European internal market by 1992, historically a great deal of change has taken place in a very short period.

Americans should be proud of the U.S. role in the birth of a united Europe. Although the United States will have to be alert to its interests as 1992 increases EC power and influence over pan-European trading policies, what George Marshall realized in 1947 is still true today: a healthy and growing European economy is in America's interest. The United States should continue to play a role in the big picture—the multilateral trading process—but it must also continue as a key player in the growth and development of regional planning—Europe 1992. America was required to think and act on both levels in 1947; to remain a world leader, the nation must maintain that dual focus.

NOTES

1. Theodore Geiger, *The Future of the International System: The United States and the World Political Economy* (Boston: Unwin Hyman, 1988), pp. 17, 25.
2. William F. Sanford, *The Marshall Plan: Origins and Implementation* (Washington, D.C.: Government Printing Office, 1987), pp. 1-3, 14.
3. Through reports and video tapes, the EC has emphasized this role; see *The European Community* (Brussels: Commission of the European Communities, 1987), p. 23.

Europe 1992: A Trading Bloc?

7

by Michael Calingaert

IMPRECISE THINKING

I find regional trading blocs a very murky concept. At the least, it appears to be characterized by imprecise thinking and terminology.

There is a popular line of thought that two important events are currently taking place that will fundamentally affect the international trading scene. One is the recent conclusion of the Free Trade Agreement between the United States and Canada. The other is the ongoing process in Europe to form a unified internal market by 1992. According to this thinking, these events represent the establishment of regional trading blocs, which in turn means that two-thirds of world trade is headed for arrangements of this type. It is further thought that in the Pacific basin, where Japan is a major player, either a trading bloc exists already or will in the near future.

The above characterization may be exaggerated, but the basic view is over-simplified and moves far too quickly from one premise to the next.

First, it is not clear to me how a regional trading bloc should be defined. What are its elements or characteristics? Is the United States, for example, a regional trading bloc? If not, is the European Community a bloc, or will it be one after 1992?

Second, are the effects created by regional trading blocs good, bad or neutral, and how is this assessment made? Then there is a general question as to whether the process of internal liberalization—whether between the United States and Canada or within the European Community, for example—is a helpful stepping stone in the direction of a more open and liberal global multilateral system. That is, will regional trading blocs help strengthen the GATT, or will they be a step toward fragmentation in a closed system? Perhaps one cannot even generalize.

Having raised these basic questions about trading blocs, I would like to explore some of the relevant issues from the perspective of the European Community. I hope that such a discussion will contribute to the development of any general theory on regional trading blocs.

THE EC AND INTERNATIONAL TRADE

Is the EC 1992 process actually happening?

EC 1992 is indeed taking place. According to one investment house in the United Kingdom, "Europe 1992 will happen, albeit slowly, because it is a historical necessity. . . . The process will also happen because it will be enforceable through the courts and because the political will exists to achieve it."

Current in all discussions of the status of EC 1992 are the two key words "momentum" and "irreversibility." There is strong political consensus and concrete support from the business community, both of which are vital to the success of EC 1992.

The Community's achievements have been remarkable. Many important steps have been taken toward the goal of a single market. These include: the decision to phase out the remaining restrictions on capital movements; the decision to phase in the recognition of academic degrees and professional qualifications obtained in other member countries; the first in a series of measures to permit the Community-wide sale of insurance from a single homebase; and the first in a series of measures to open up procurement by government entities.

How the program will evolve is still a question mark. A number of very tough issues remain, and their resolution will be difficult as the conflicting interests within the European Community become increasingly relevant. Nonetheless, the 1992 process, on the whole, is well under way. A very different European Community is being created, whether it will be completed in 1992 or, as more likely, at some point later during the 1990s.

How will EC 1992 affect the European Community's trade policy and actions?

One should bear in mind that to some extent there already is a common trade policy. The Community's executive arm, the European Commission, is responsible for trade negotiations and other activities in the GATT. The delegation from the European Commission speaks on behalf of the entire European Community. Of course, the European Commission's activities are based on the mandate, or instructions, that have been given to it by the member states. As in other policy issues in the Community, these instructions result from a process of voting and consensus building among the member states.

The clearest place to see the extent to which the EC is a regional trading bloc—or how 1992 will affect external trade—is at the outer border of the European Community. Consider first the common external tariff. No massive change in the level of tariff protection is being talked about. In any event, this is less important than it has been in the past as tariff levels around the world have been significantly reduced. There may be a small degree of tariff adjustment—some upward offset by some downward—but on the whole no real change should take place as a result of EC 1992.

Another interesting, but more controversial, area relates to quotas and other quantitative restrictions, especially in the two areas of automobiles and textiles. Basically, the EC has to decide—and it should be very difficult—either how to adapt the approximately 1,000 quotas imposed by individual member countries on specific countries around the world to a system of common EC quotas or how to phase them out.

Undoubtedly, some of the existing quotas will be phased out. At the same time, some will undoubtedly be extended on an EC-wide basis. Automobiles are a case in point. Countries, particularly France and Italy, that have very tight import controls on automobiles are not likely in the near or medium term to become part of a European-wide system where the protection would be far less than now prevails. In addition, international trade in textiles, which is governed by the Multi-Fiber Agreement, is most unlikely to be significantly liberalized in the next few years.

A third area involving the EC's external borders is antidumping and the related issue of rules of origin. Recently, there has been a very aggressive and restrictive policy on the part of the European Community in the antidumping area. The European Commission hotly rejects the claim that the rules on antidumping have been consciously changed by policy decision. Rather, it maintains that it is carrying out legitimate, existing EC regulations. Nevertheless, the EC has recently made greater use of antidumping procedures in its trade relations with the Asian countries. It is premature, however, to identify long-term trends.

The issue of rules of origin is the subject of much discussion in the European Community. What constitutes an import from a particular country and how is it distinguished from a domestically produced product when part of the manufacturing process takes place abroad and part occurs inside the Community? This is not an easy issue to resolve, but its significance for trade is not inconsiderable.

How will the European Community function internally as a unit and to what extent will it be a bloc?

Perhaps the first place to look for answers is in standards. Certainly, the multiplicity of standards has been a major source of the fragmentation within the EC. As a result, serious efforts are now under way to try to harmonize standards inside the Community. The questions that need to be addressed include: How will this be done? To what extent will harmonization be a transparent process? To what extent will outsiders participate in the process? The EC standards that are ultimately adopted will, of course, be of major concern to outsiders.

Another very important area is procurement by public entities, which has been highly regulated at the national level. One of the goals of the EC 1992 program is to open up public procurement within the Community to a far greater extent. The hope is to make it a much more transparent process. Many so-called national champions are going to be adversely affected by this shift, which would create enormous potential for nonnational firms. Clearly, this will be an area to watch in terms of what measures the EC ultimately adopts, how they are put into effect and how long this process takes.

Incentives for inward investment are also of concern. There certainly are indications that efforts are being made within the EC to make it more difficult for outsiders to operate from outside the Community. In other words, the goal is to bring more investment into the European Community. Many multinational company investment plans obviously will be dictated primarily by market considerations. Given a single unit of 320 million people, there are many very valid market reasons why companies will want to operate from inside rather than outside the EC. However, one may still wonder about what is behind some antidumping and rules of origin policies and actions taken by the European Community. A case in point, of course, was the decision that the diffusion process on semiconductors had to take place inside the European Community in order for semiconductors to qualify as EC products under the rules of origin. In addition, there are questions as to how European competition policy will be carried out. It is also significant that a substantial program of EC-wide research and development is under way.

What will be the net impact of the EC 1992 program in terms of international trade?

There is a long-standing debate on whether the results of regional agreements produce more trade creation or trade diversion. However, no clear-cut or generally accepted answers have come from this debate to indicate the possible net effects from, say, the creation of an internal market in the European Community. Certainly, there will be an increase in the general level of growth under any circumstances. Whether it is 7 percent—the optimum postulated in the Cecchini report (the only comprehensive analysis to date of the impact of completing the internal market)—or somewhat less spectacular growth, there is bound to be a higher level of economic activity.

In addition, trade theorists often assume that the cost of intra-EC trade will decline. One of the studies conducted by Alistair Smith and Anthony Venables as part of the Cecchini report calculates a 2.5 percent drop, which it calls a conservative figure. My guess, and it is not more than that, is that this is a conservative figure.

Richard Cawley and Michael Davenport, in another section of the Cecchini study, estimate that the direct effect of the removal of internal barriers will be to reduce imports from outside the EC by about 2 percent; if the decline in the cost of production that such a reduction produces is added in, they estimate a further drop in imports of 5.7 to 7.7 percent. Similar estimates by Smith and Venables postulate that an increase in competition will reduce prices, which will cause a further reduction in imports.

The problem with all these estimates is that they are made using static analysis. Often such predictions do not allow for other dynamic trade effects. They do not take into account changing trade among members of the European Community and, more important, between the EC and the outside world. In any event, I believe the outside world will benefit from most of the changes that are taking place inside the European Community.

What are the implications of EC 1992 for the GATT negotiations?

One should try, at least conceptually, to look at EC 1992 within the context of the Uruguay Round (and also perhaps farther down the road in terms of post-Uruguay Round trading relationships). The interrelationship between the Uruguay Round and EC 1992 is difficult to sort out. In an ideal world, the two processes would reinforce each other. Certainly, multilateral moves toward liberalization through the Uruguay Round will help determine the outcome of EC 1992.

But clearly the priority inside the Community—to the extent that priorities have to be set—is that EC 1992 comes first. As far as most Europeans are concerned, the Uruguay Round is second in importance. There are some cases where decisions taken in the context of EC 1992 have been helpful to the Uruguay Round (for example, in the areas of public procurement and intellectual property rights). In their internal process, the Europeans began with some general policies and, on the basis of these policies, proposed directives that were placed on the table inside the European Community. Once this was done, the EC then proceeded in the Uruguay Round in a much more forthcoming way.

After this current round of GATT talks, we will likely see more cohesion in terms of EC action and activity in the GATT. Greater confidence and greater strength will be shown by the EC. Parenthetically, in terms of American interests, that may or may not be good. But my expectation is that the EC will remain essentially outward looking, a reflection of self-interest as determined by the partners within the Community.

Service sector issues are very relevant in this context. There are currently no GATT rules in this area, so the outcome of the Uruguay Round negotiations on services will significantly affect the EC's receptivity to nonmember firms.

In this connection, it is troublesome that the European Community has continued to push the concept of reciprocity. For example, at the December 1988 Montreal GATT meeting, the EC tried to insert language that would permit the use of reciprocity in opening up service markets. This is a prime example of potential difficulties.

In the past, we have tended to follow the so-called national treatment principle, i.e., foreign companies can establish operations in, say, America and be treated as American companies. Under national treatment, American and EC banking firms, for example, could function under very different standards in the EC and U.S. markets. The newer reciprocity concept states that the EC and American banking firms should operate under the same general rules in both markets.

The European Community has made it clear that it intends to use its reciprocity rules to create leverage. Thus, it may be a question of not simply maintaining the existing level of protection, but also raising it in certain cases.

Is the EC a trading bloc?

Because so many questions remain, my conclusions are fairly tame. Obviously, EC 1992 will be far different from the Community of 1982 or even of 1989. The implications of EC 1992 for the world trading system are unclear because decisions are still being taken and policies are being worked out within the EC.

I suppose the European Community after 1992 will be a regional trading bloc by definition. But that is not necessarily, or inherently, a more restrictive situation than the status quo. The outcome of the EC 1992 program will depend on many factors, both internal and external. It is possible that creation of a single European market will give rise to protectionist forces inside the EC. Some Europeans may say, "Now that there is a real market of 320 million people, we are much better off than before, and we should not worry too much about opening up to the outside world." Such a view will be fueled by problems of internal dislocation due to EC 1992 changes. In the final analysis, how the success of EC 1992 is perceived by Europeans will be important—will it be seen to provide more benefits to outsiders, such as the United States or Japan, or to insiders?

Clearly, however, the more open the European Community—or the European regional trading bloc—the greater the advantages to the EC and to the rest of the world.

THE HISTORICAL PERSPECTIVE

One reason for imprecise thinking about EC 1992 and regional trading blocs is that analysts sometimes lack a historical background concerning the European Community. In addition, they sometimes confuse the major parts of the EC 1992 program.[1]

Toward a Single Market

The basis for the 1992 program is the 1957 Treaty of Rome that established the EC. The treaty set as a goal the formation of a common market, to be achieved by removal of tariffs and quantitative restrictions between the member states and of measures having equivalent effect. In addition, the treaty called for the abolition of obstacles to the free movement of services, people and capital. The elimination of internal tariffs was achieved by 1968. However, progress in other areas was limited, and during the 1970s the difficulty of removing or reducing barriers was exacerbated by an unfavorable economic climate characterized by sluggish growth, high unemployment and inflationary pressures, in part the result of the two oil shocks.

By the early 1980s, pressures were growing for the EC to attack the various problems that had left it in a state of "Eurosclerosis." These pressures resulted from three interrelated concerns: the indifferent state of the EC economy and its structural rigidities; the perception that the EC was falling behind due to competition from the United States and particularly Japan (especially in the high technology field); and the gridlock in decision-making on key issues.

These pressures came not only from within EC institutions but, more important, from the EC business community, which increasingly recognized that the fragmentation of the EC's market significantly raised costs and thus reduced its opportunities both in the EC and in what was increasingly becoming a global economy. Indeed, reference was made with growing persistence to the costs of "non-Europe."

A final contributing factor to the program's launch was the arrival at the European Commission in 1985 of Jacques Delors as president and Lord Cockfield as the commissioner responsible for the internal market. Delors was determined that the Commission should undertake a major initiative to regenerate the Community, and he selected as the vehicle the completion of the internal market. For his part, Cockfield proved to be a dogged and effective promoter and executor of the 1992 program.

In 1985, the EC issued a White Paper that contained the plan of the European Community to "complete the internal market" by removing the barriers to the free movement of goods, services, people, and capital among the 12 member states. The White Paper brought together for the first time a comprehensive listing of the measures deemed necessary for achieving the goal of a single integrated market and included a timetable for action on each individual measure, with the entire process scheduled for completion by the end of 1992.

The Institutional Framework

Any assessment of developments toward 1992 must take account of the relevant EC institutions and the changing nature of their interrelationship. Traditionally, the two main bodies have been the Council and the Commission. The Council, on which all 12 EC member states are represented, is the supreme decision-making body, while the Commission drafts proposals for Council decision and carries out policies established by the EC.

However, two major changes were effected by the adoption of the Single European Act in 1987. First, whereas virtually all Council decisions relating to the internal market had previously required unanimity, most of them can now be reached on the basis of weighted majority voting. This change will undoubtedly enable the Council to reach decisions more easily as well as introduce a greater degree of alliance building among the member states.

Second, the act increased the powers of the European Parliament, the only democratically established body of the Community. Consisting of 518 directly elected members who sit in political—not national—groups, the European Parliament's original limited powers were essentially those of delaying legislation. Under the Single European Act, Parliament was given a more direct decision-making role. Its views on Commission proposals have to be considered in the redrafting stage, and amendments to proposed legislation passed by an absolute majority cannot be overturned by the Council except by unanimity. As a result of Parliament's increased importance, the dynamics of the relationship among these three institutions were bound to change, with one occasionally seeking to play the remaining two against each other.

A fourth institution, the European Court of Justice, also plays a major role. With powers similar to those of the U.S. Supreme Court, the European Court has contributed to the process of economic integration by overturning a number of national government measures impeding the free flow of goods and services. It will undoubtedly be increasingly called upon to ensure that member state actions conform to the Treaty of Rome and Community legislation.

CONTENT OF THE 1992 PROGRAM

The barriers to the single market that are addressed in the White Paper can be divided into eight categories.

(1) *Border controls.* In view of the differences among the member states in indirect taxation (value added and excise taxes), plant and animal health regulations and import restrictions, border controls are maintained to ensure that the laws and regulations of the importing country are respected and thereby to prevent competitive distortions. In addition, borders have become increasingly important in controlling illegal immigration and in combating terrorism and drug trafficking.

(2) *Limitation on the freedom of movement of people and their right of establishment.* Although member state citizens are free to move from one EC country to another for work, most member states have imposed restrictions on the recognition of academic degrees and professional qualifications acquired elsewhere in the Community. As a result, professionals have often encountered difficulties in practicing their profession in other member states.

(3) *Different indirect taxation regimes.* Although all EC members have adopted systems of value added taxation, the rates and coverage vary considerably from country to country, and the variation in the incidence of excise tax is even greater. To prevent competitive distortions, the EC has followed a system for internal EC trade of rebating taxation at the border and imposing the tax of the importing country.

(4) *Lack of a common legal framework.* To a considerable extent, the operations of enterprises are governed by national, rather than Community, regulations; thus, cross-border business is more complicated and difficult than it would be in an integrated market. For intellectual property, there are as yet no EC-wide patents, trademarks or copyrights.

(5) *Controls on movement of capital.* Although full freedom of capital movement has been achieved in a few member states, restrictions of varying intensity remain in most countries, particularly for short-term capital movements and activities of individuals.

(6) *Regulation of services.* The service sector is, on the whole, highly regulated by national governments. This is particularly the case for financial services, but transportation and broadcasting are also subject to considerable regulation.

(7) *Divergent regulations and technical standards.* For the most part, sellers in the EC market must conform to the regulations and standards applicable in the individual countries. This adds immeasurably to the cost and complexity of doing business in the Community.

(8) *Public procurement policies.* To an overwhelming extent, contracts are awarded by public entities in the EC to firms of the country in question. In addition, energy, telecommunications, transportation, and water supply are exempt from EC public procurement regulations. The net result is massive inefficiencies in a significant sector of the EC economy.

PROGRESS AND PROSPECTS

At an indeterminate point early in 1988, the EC's 1992 program took off. Whereas the mood in the Community had ranged from cautious optimism to healthy skepticism, the consensus now is clearly that the process is under way. As one observer put it, "whereas we were pushing the ball uphill, it is now going downhill and the only question is the angle of the slope." Popular enthusiasm is high; governments are emphasizing the importance of EC 1992 to their citizens; and businesses, increasingly convinced that 1992 will happen, are acting on their convictions and thereby helping to make it happen. A remarkable degree of political consensus has been achieved, and it is rare for a mainstream European politician to profess anything other than total support for the effort.

Progress toward completion of the internal market can be measured quantitatively by the number of proposals submitted by the Commission to the Council and the number of measures the Council has adopted. Although the White Paper called for the Commission to have submitted all of its proposals by the end of 1988, the Commission is around the 90 percent mark. The Council has completed action on about one-third of the proposals—mostly the less controversial measures. Nevertheless, this represents reasonably good progress.

A qualitative assessment is more difficult to make, particularly because the Commission has consciously refused to set priorities among the measures requiring action. However, the key areas are probably the elimination of border controls, the opening up of the public procurement market, the harmonization of regulations and technical standards, and the liberalization of capital movements and financial services. In addressing these issues, the Commission has wisely eschewed attempts—which characterized past (largely unsuccessful) efforts—to legislate Community-wide provisions. Rather, it has emphasized deregulation and the mutual recognition of member states' laws and regulations.

The situation and prospects for the categories of barriers are outlined below.

(1) *Border controls.* Despite the symbolic and tangible costs of maintaining these controls, little progress has been made toward their removal, and prospects for such action by 1992 are slight. Efforts to approximate indirect tax regimes have met with strong resistance from many member states; the Commission is behind schedule in presenting proposals for the harmonization of plant and animal health regulations, and member states have not pressed vigorously for resolution of the outstanding issues; few steps have been taken to eliminate national import restrictions or to extend them on an EC-wide basis; and many states have been reluctant to consider alternatives to border protection in the areas of immigration, drugs and terrorism.

(2) *Professional qualifications.* Despite the extreme sensitivity of this issue, particularly in the more developed member states, the foot-dragging that had characterized deliberations on harmonization of qualifications in specific sectors, and the requirement for a unanimous decision, the Council agreed in 1988 to phase out restrictions by 1990. With some exceptions, member states will be obligated to accept academic degrees and professional qualifications acquired in other member states, a significant psychological step forward even if the rights conferred will be used only to a limited extent. Two areas remaining for action, however, are restrictions on the right of citizens to live in other member states for purposes other than work and mutual recognition (or other provisions) for the vocational professions.

(3) *Taxation.* Despite efforts by the Commission to move member states toward acceptance of ranges for two categories of value added tax and of common rates for excise taxes, the opposition has been intense, and not surprisingly so. The power to levy taxes is a jealously guarded prerogative of national governments and will not be lightly given up. But on a more immediate, practical basis, the proposed changes would significantly affect national government revenue. Even though the proposed ranges or rates are largely based on averages of member state taxes, the adjustments that would be required in many cases would drastically affect tax receipts and/or the mix between direct and indirect taxes, to say nothing of the effect on excise taxes that have been adopted either to promote the consumption of domestic products or to impose "sin taxes" on certain products.

(4) *Legal framework.* Some movement has taken place on company law issues. However, the increasing attention being given (particularly within the Commission) to the "social agenda"—covering the panoply of worker interest issues that range from institutionalization of labor-management contacts and safety measures in the workplace to worker participation on company boards and EC-wide collective bargaining—will probably make progress more difficult. Although action is presently blocked on establishing EC-wide trademark and patent systems, these will likely be achieved before 1992. Work on copyrights has begun only recently. One area of intense Commission activity is competition policy, particularly relevant in the context of sharply increased merger and acquisition activity. Agreement will probably be reached in the near future on Commission powers to regulate cross-border EC mergers. In addition, the Commission will be active in limiting state aids by member governments and entities.

(5) *Capital movement.* A crucial component of the single market will be complete freedom of the movement of capital. The Community took a major decision in mid-1988 when it agreed to phase out all remaining restrictions—for the eight major countries by 1990, for Spain and Ireland by 1992 and for Greece and Portugal by 1995 at the latest. In all probability, this decision will put pressure on the weaker EC currencies, for which some protection is available in two forms: an EC "safety net" fund and the possibility of reinstituting controls under tightly specified conditions. To deal with potential capital movement problems resulting from efforts to minimize tax burdens and/or evade taxation, the Commission was obligated to make proposals regarding the different taxation regimes on unearned income, and the Council was committed to act on them by mid-1989. But due to the lack of consensus, this effort was abandoned.

(6) *Regulation of services.* Recognizing the importance of liberalizing the service sector, the Commission is concentrating on removing barriers to the provision of services in member states and across borders. In financial services, the proposed approach consists of deregulation of operations, harmonization of the essential standards for supervision, mutual recognition among member states of those standards, and "home country control" (i.e., supervision of operations by the authorities in the country of establishment of the institution in question, irrespective of where the operations are carried out). A measure establishing an EC-wide banking regime based on this approach was adopted in late 1989. Similar proposals are under consideration for insurance and the operation of stock exchanges. Progress will be slow in transportation, although a major decision liberalizing road transportation was taken in mid-1988, and a start has been made on air transportation.

(7) *Regulations and standards.* A "new approach" to standard setting has been undertaken that limits harmonization to the establishment of "essential requirements." Pending the establishment of standards by the relevant European standards bodies, member states will recognize other members' standards as long as they conform to these essential requirements. Although the physical volume of work is considerable, those involved think the process is working well. Still, many questions remain, such as the degree of transparency in the process, the nature of the standards that will be ultimately adopted, and whether foreign testing and certification bodies will be recognized by EC authorities.

(8) *Public procurement.* The Commission is moving aggressively to pry open the market of purchases by public entities that account for as much as 15 percent of the EC's gross domestic product. Agreement has been reached on rules regarding supply contracts, and a companion measure on public works contracts is under discussion and will likely be approved reasonably soon. The Commission has also introduced a proposal to apply EC procurement rules to the four "excluded sectors." In addition, the Commission is considering how to overcome the insufficient redress available for aggrieved parties and its own insufficient enforcement powers. Important measures on public procurement will probably have been adopted by 1992, but significant sectors of the economy will be adversely affected and thus can be expected to impede implementation.

OBSTACLES

Despite an impressive start and widespread enthusiastic support, the EC 1992 program faces very considerable obstacles that will not magically disappear. To begin with, the differences among the cultures, languages and traditions of the member states go back many centuries and will necessarily affect attitudes and actions. Although forces are at work in the direction of greater homogeneity, change will be generational and only marginally subject to government action.

Apart from these underlying differences, the issues addressed in the White Paper are complex and difficult to resolve. Invariably, they will be perceived by one or another group, sector or country as putting their interests at risk. In addition, issues are linked in many cases, so that a decision on one issue will necessitate resolving another, often equally thorny, issue. Furthermore, the 1992 program necessarily involves a continued transfer of authority from the national governments to EC institutions in Brussels. Although national sovereignty is not a major issue, sensitivities remain a potential impediment to EC 1992.

Nevertheless, the question now is not whether the European Community will move toward a single market, but rather how far and how quickly. "Euro-phoria" masks a number of doubts and fears as well as difficulties in achieving the 1992 goal. Regardless, the EC of 1992 will be considerably different from that of 1985 or even that of today. It behooves the United States to pay close attention to developments and to seek to influence them in directions that promote U.S. interests. The results of EC 1992 will not only influence conditions within the European Community, but will also have a major impact on the future of the international trading system.

NOTES

1. For more details and analysis, see Michael Calingaert, *The 1992 Challenge from Europe: Development of the European Community's Internal Market* (Washington, D.C.: National Planning Association, 1988).

Regional Trade and Trends: A North American View from the Inside Out

8

by Maureen A. Farrow and Robert C. York

Changes are taking place in the world economy that are forcing national governments to sit up and take note. Witness the growing awareness of the finite limits of the world's environment, the technological advances that are shaping industrial structure, an aging population that will lead to major increases in the cost of social programs, shifts in world incomes and economic imbalances, and the attention being given to policy coordination.

The renewed and growing interest in the trend toward regional trade liberalization—or regional trading blocs—is another example. This change is different, however, because the wheels are in motion, but nobody knows which way they are spinning. Is the world headed for a series of separate trading blocs? If so, does this threaten to undermine, or even destroy, the multilateral trading system? Is the General Agreement on Tariffs and Trade already dead? What are the implications of these issues for future Canadian and U.S. trade policies?

OVERVIEW

The first section of this discussion outlines some of the forces of change in the world economy that are responsible for the increasing interest in regional trade liberalization. These changes have created much uncertainty about the direction of the world trading system. Attention is focused particularly on macroeconomic imbalances in the world economy, structural shifts (that is, microeconomic events), globalization, and the precarious condition of the Uruguay Round of the GATT.

The next section examines the trend toward regional trading blocs, best exemplified by the U.S.-Canada Free Trade Agreement, by European economic integration in 1992 and, to a lesser extent, by closer cooperation among the Pacific Rim countries. The North American reactions to the events discussed in the first section are considered as well as the motives for the FTA from both the Canadian and U.S. perspectives.

The final section sets out the implications of the FTA and EC 1992 as harbingers of serious moves toward other regional trading blocs. The trade policy implications for Canada and the United States are also spelled out.

TRENDS AND CHANGES IN THE WORLD ECONOMY

Macroeconomic Factors

Macroeconomic factors that can no longer be separated easily from microeconomic factors or industrial structure have dramatically shifted global balances—or, more correctly, they have created global imbalances. These factors include the twin deficits in the United States, the trade surpluses of Japan and the Asian newly industrializing economies (NIEs), the high unemployment in Europe, and the debt crisis and stagnation in the developing countries.

The U.S. story is by now quite familiar. The rapid growth of the U.S. economy from the depths of the recession in 1981-82 and the marked appreciation of the U.S. dollar to unprecedented heights contributed to the deficit in the U.S. current account. The high propensity of Americans to consume and their corresponding low rate of savings, combined with an expansionary fiscal policy and a mismatch between revenues and expenditures, created a relatively attractive financial climate for international investment funds. Within a few years, the United States had moved from being the world's largest net creditor to the world's largest net debtor. In short, the United States and, to a large extent, Canada have enjoyed a five- to six-year spending binge financed by foreigners.

According to mainstream economists' views, the trade deficit originates mainly in the current account; thus, reducing this deficit is a matter of quicker expansion in the rest of the world and a significant reduction in the U.S. fiscal deficit. The "naive" policy prescription, and that of the Reagan Administration, was to let the current account improve through the J-curve—that is, through currency depreciation. (We call this prescription naive because it did not fully appreciate the structural imbalances in the world economy that are explained below.) This spurred calls for macropolicy coordination among the G-7 economies. (Indeed, 30 prominent economists from 13 countries issued a statement in Washington in December 1987 supporting policy coordination.) It also spurred calls from protectionist factions in the U.S. Congress for defensive trade policies and led to finger-pointing at unfair trade practices abroad. These calls resulted in the watered-down, but in our view still potent, Omnibus Trade and Competitiveness Act of 1988—potent because it contains some measures designed to allow the United States to adopt unilateral definitions of unfair trade practices.

The mainstream view of how to solve the global imbalance is increasingly called into question for two reasons. First, Krugman, among others, has reinvestigated the view held by Feldstein and Horioka regarding the precise link between savings and investment and the fiscal and current account deficits.[1] While it is accepted that reducing the U.S. fiscal deficit is important, Krugman's research suggests that it is also important to examine structural elements such as the low U.S. savings rate and the low level of labor productivity.

Second, policy coordination involving the reduction of U.S. bilateral trade surpluses, particularly with Japan, West Germany and the Asian NIEs, does not seem to have worked. In the case of Japan, the surplus has been reduced, but the net effect on the U.S. trade balance has been small. Both of these factors suggest that U.S. and Canadian policymakers should turn more attention to microeconomic policies that address the competitiveness issue and, at the same time, should place a higher priority on trade policy.

Hence, there are implications here for the world trading system—all of which can be positive. Fostering a spurt of import growth in Japan and the Asian NIEs will solve only about one-third of the U.S. trade imbalance. A significant narrowing of the current account requires much more in the way of a multilateral shift in world trade patterns, which lends support to more liberalized multilateral trade practices.

There is another factor that should predispose U.S. long-range planners to advocate a healthy, functioning GATT. As long as Gramm-Rudman has effect and the U.S. fiscal deficit is brought down, the U.S. current account will turn toward surplus or even into surplus in the 1990s because a large trade surplus will be required to service the accumulated net foreign liabilities. Thus, the world trade system might benefit from the shifts in world macroeconomic conditions. There will be pressure for rational governments to liberalize trade through multilateral arrangements and reduce unfair trade practices, rather than to resort to trade wars and to erect trade barriers. However, there is a cautionary note on trade policy. Global imbalances might also be dealt with through bilateral agreements and even through regional trading arrangements; both would have serious consequences for the multilateral trading system.

Microeconomic Factors

There have been growing indications of structural imbalances as well as macroeconomic imbalances in the global economy. These imbalances are related to microeconomic factors that affect industrial structure—such as taxation, regulation, technology, and research and development. The low savings rates and low levels of total factor productivity in the countries with fiscal and current account deficits—namely, Canada and the United States—suggest that macro factors are not the whole story. There can be little argument that capital inflows, exchange rate appreciation and accommodative U.S. fiscal policies created the problems in the United States. But there is also growing agreement about the extent to which these problems were, and continue to be, exacerbated by other underlying factors—most importantly, competitiveness.

U.S. and Canadian total factor productivity has been growing very slowly relative to their foreign competitors and relative to their own past performance. Much of the income growth in these economies is due to increases in the labor force and not to productivity. The Organization for Economic Cooperation and Development estimates that total factor productivity in the U.S. grew by 1.5 percent in the pre-1973 period and not at all in the 1979-85 period. Labor productivity in the United States over the same two periods grew by 2.2 and 0.6 percent, respectively. This has serious implications for the U.S. standard of living—productivity determines real wages, and real wages are a large component of national income.

Hatsopoulos et al. argue that the United States is no longer home of the leading edge industries, where many spillovers filter down throughout the economy to boost economic growth.[2] Instead, they argue that the product cycle now more likely begins in Japan and/or the Asian NIEs with the introduction of a new product that is later emulated by U.S. firms and industries. Earlier work by Scott recognized this shift and offers a solution to the U.S. competitiveness problem.[3] He argues that restoring U.S. competitiveness requires systemic changes that affect economic activity at the factory, firm and industry level as well as government micro- and macroeconomic policies. In short, Scott supports a model, based on the export success of Japan and the Asian NIEs, that is coming more and more into fashion. This theory is independent of the classical paradigms of international trade theory based on Ricardian comparative advantage and is based instead on the ability of government to "shape comparative advantage" in "strategic industries" and through "strategic trade policy."

The Industrial Policy School, as it is now known, prescribes an interventionist policy directed at attracting "sunrise" or leading edge industries—those with large and beneficial spillover effects and which yield pure economic rents over a long period of time.[4] These industries do not depend on factor endowments to bestow comparative advantage, but acquire it through targeted microeconomic policies (e.g., industrial subsidies, tax incentives and regulation) and import protection until such industries mature. The most celebrated case in point is the Japanese semiconductor industry.[5]

Despite its obvious appeal, the Industrial Policy School view is rife with difficulties. Among them are: how does the government pick winners? Why should the government be able to identify and back winners better than the market? And, important from the perspective of this chapter, how great is the potential for trade friction and retaliation?

The proponents of industrial policy activism seem to imply a passive response by the country's trading partners. This seems naive. In a simple two-country model, it is not hard to imagine a situation where both countries simultaneously support and protect their domestic industries. This would lead to a fall in the volume of trade and world income and a rise in domestic costs relative to a world where both countries resist protection and are better off for it.[6] Although this approach is appealing to individual countries, it would wreak havoc in the world trading system.

Globalization

One of the most profound changes in economic activity in this decade has been the increasing globalization of many product markets and services, particularly financial services. The term "globalization" refers generally to a marketplace for standardized products that is worldwide in nature.[7] It relies on economies of scale in production, distribution, marketing, and management. It also has important implications for the volume of world trade and the patterns of trade. This is best demonstrated by Professor John Helliwell who suggests that the "longer term trade balance changes are likely to come not from Japanese imports of standard U.S. goods, but from the establishment of plants outside Japan to make 'Japanese' goods for Japanese and world consumption."[8]

What does globalization mean for a large economy like the U.S. and, importantly, for a small economy like Canada? Helliwell sees globalization as an opportunity to exploit; to be successful, countries must remain flexible enough to adapt to change and view it as an opportunity rather than a threat. As Helliwell puts it:

> [Indeed] the biggest risks [of globalization] are probably posed by national policies that react defensively to protect declining activities, or to subsidize new activities, in a mutually costly attempt to compete with similarly subsidized activities in other countries. The risks are to the international [trading] system itself as well as to the economic health of the individual countries adopting such strategies.

> If national policies could embrace and exploit the inevitable globalization of economic activities, this will permit the removal, even if gradually, of a number of the more wasteful and debilitating national or regional policies, designed in the mistaken hope that "defense" or "counter-attack" is a feasible strategy for any country, and especially a relatively small and open one like Canada, to respond to changes in the global economy.[9]

Helliwell also summarizes well the implications of globalization for the world trading system and for regional trading blocs. In the case of Japan, Helliwell articulates the view that innovative countries can "go it alone" and can prosper in doing so.

> From the global context, perhaps Japan has been so successful because the need for and benefits of globalization have been more obvious there. While the countries of the EEC were opening doors to each other, and reaping the undoubted benefits therefrom, they were often cementing their unity at the expense of less opening up to the rest of the world. Japan, being a major industrial block, was opening up to the entire world, and finding, as might be expected, that trade can be most beneficial among countries with very different incomes and resources. While Europe and North America each have about 5 percent of the world's population, South and East Asia have over 50 percent, and Japan is becoming the center of that fast-growing area. With 5 percent of Asia's population and 50 percent of Asia's GNP, i.e., with real incomes ten times as high as those in the continent as a whole, Japan might well have been threatened by the threat of low wage competition; but by accepting these differences as providing opportunities rather than threats, the Japanese have been able to enjoy the real income advantages of a high yen while still maintaining an enviable rate of growth of domestic output and employment. This is not an advertisement for Japan, but merely cited as a partial example to show how the benefits of accepting and anticipating globalization are not pie in the sky, but are there to be found by those who are able and willing to face the risks and seize the opportunities.[10]

If we understand Helliwell correctly, we must view globalization as a real push for the multilateral trading system through the GATT. It will force countries to examine their business climates relative to other countries that are competing for investment and leading edge industries. This climate is defined by factors such as access to world markets and domestic micro- and macroeconomic policies. This means that mutually beneficial harmonization of national policies might be implemented in areas such as taxation and the treatment of capital formation. Such an environment also lends itself to international cooperation. These matters can be handled through an effective, functioning multilateral trading system—a system that, for example, reduces trade barriers, provides means to resolve trade disputes, protects investment from discrimination, and establishes rules for trade in services.

The Uruguay Round of the GATT

Arguably the most successful of all the international institutions established after World War II, the GATT has presided since 1947 over major reductions in trade barriers that have been accompanied by dramatic increases in world trade. The GATT is now at a pivotal stage in its history. Many observers see the current Uruguay Round of negotiations as critical to the future of the world trading system. The outcome of the round cannot yet be foreseen. Some observers remain optimistic that it will achieve significant gains; others fear that the GATT will be unable to maintain even the present degree of liberalized trade. Still others contend that if the multilateral route fails, or yields only small gains, the United States may opt for a series of bilateral arrangements similar to the FTA.[11]

The likelihood of any success in the round will depend on the objectives, expectations and, in many cases, the concessions that contracting parties are willing to make. Previous rounds of negotiations have had specific themes. For example, the Kennedy Round (1963-67) addressed tariffs and the Tokyo Round (1973-79) focused on nontariff barriers. The current Uruguay Round is ambitious—perhaps comparable in scope and coverage only to the 1947 Havana Conference that started it all.

The Uruguay Round covers 15 negotiating areas, including the so-called new areas of trade in textiles and in services, trade-related intellectual property rights, investment, agriculture, and important measures aimed at strengthening the GATT as an institution.

Active participation among contracting parties has never been greater, and developing countries are beginning to play a vital role. Many like-minded countries have aligned themselves in coalitions, such as the Cairns and de la Paix groups, that articulate their needs, make suggestions and pressure the more prominent players into keeping the talks moving. They also help bridge the gap between industrial and developing countries. The importance of this function cannot be overlooked since the future of the multilateral trading system is dependent on the active participation and cooperation of the developing countries.

The round is now in the final period of negotiations, and although there has been substantial progress in some areas, the four key issues—intellectual property rights, textiles, safeguards, and agricultural subsidies—remain unresolved. Sylvia Ostry, Canada's Ambassador to the GATT, suggests that progress is possible if contracting parties would "catalyze momentum in the Round on issues which will increase private sector support in the industrialized countries and most of all in the United States."[12] She refers primarily to the "new" issues, particularly services and intellectual property, and possibly investment, which are complex and extremely contentious areas for some developing nations.

Ostry and Smith also think that the current difficulties between conflicting national objectives could be quelled by negotiations of like-minded countries for a conditional most-favored-nation clause.[13] This clause would allow countries willing to adhere to its terms to enjoy the benefit of clear trading rules, while also allowing for the potential participation of other countries over time. Both authors, although recognizing that this creates the danger of a "super-GATT," prefer it to a watered-down round that in the long term provokes more trade frictions, and perhaps more bilateral or regional arrangements.

REGIONAL TRADE LIBERALIZATION

Is the trend toward regional trade liberalization—or regional trading blocs—on the move? The implementation of the U.S.-Canada FTA and the desire for economic integration in the European Community by 1992 might suggest that the trend is gaining momentum. The movement to liberalize trade through regional groupings now covers 71 countries, including all the advanced industrial countries except Japan. Whether this trend is due to the failure of the GATT to contain the current level of protectionism, let alone roll it back, to the evolution of the world trading system itself, or to the realization that large markets really matter is open to meaningful discussion. We confine our remarks here mainly to the case of North America and the FTA and the motivations underlying its initiation and inception.

The Stage Is Set

The FTA has its roots deep in Canada-U.S. economic history, beginning with the Reciprocity Treaty in 1874. Then came two significant trade liberalizing agreements in the 1930s, free trade in agricultural machinery and implements in 1944 that has carried through to the present time, and the Automotive Products Trade Agreement (auto pact) in 1965, a centerpiece of Canadian commercial policy and a symbol of Canada-U.S. trade relations.

However, the free trade agreement now in place is only partly the result of history and the long-standing economic relationship between the world's largest trading partners. The motivations underlying the FTA arose mostly from events and attitudes that were dissimilar on each side of the border.

Canada Reacts. There were three underlying reasons for Canada's free trade initiative with the United States. First, Canada is a small open economy that depends on exports for nearly 30 percent of its income and employment. Before the FTA, it was the only developed country outside Australia and New Zealand that did not have free access to a market of at least 100 million consumers. Thus, with a domestic population of a mere 25 million people, Canada lacked a market large enough to realize economies of scale and specialization. Free trade with the United States offered Canadian industry an opportunity to rationalize its production and to become more competitive in an increasingly competitive international marketplace.

Second, three-quarters of all Canadian exports are destined for the U.S. market. So not only is access to the U.S. market of concern to Canadian exporters, but security of access is critical too. However, that access was threatened by a rising tide of U.S. protectionism in the early 1980s and the U.S. policy of "administered protection" through trade remedy laws and the widespread use of voluntary restraint agreements and other measures. In addition, the aggressive approach of the Reagan Administration in protecting domestic import-competing sectors often caught up Canada in actions aimed chiefly at others.[14] Thus, a bilateral agreement with the United States offered Canadian exporters security of access by reducing risks inherent in the unilateral interpretation and application of U.S. trade remedy laws and the power of the U.S. Congress to pass protectionist legislation affecting Canada.

Third, chief Canadian negotiator Simon Reisman pointed to a coincidence of the typically cyclical nature of Canadian and U.S. political and business attitudes toward trade liberalization.[15] When the Canadian economy is booming, Canadians tend to look inward and subsequently engage in nationalist economic policies including restraint of trade. When times turn bad, they look outward to export markets to cure their woes. The United States, Reisman observed, has a similar but reverse cycle: the U.S. looks outward in times of prosperity and inward when the economy slumps. The recession of 1981-82 was preceded by a period that synchronized this trade policy cycle. The United States rebounded quickly from the recession and looked outward, as did Canada when its economy did not respond quite so quickly. The result was support for bilateral free trade with the United States from political quarters and the business community, the latter group supporting the initiative for the first time in Canadian economic history.

The U.S. Responds. On the U.S. side, the motivations for picking up on Canada's lead were twofold. First, in the early 1980s, the United States was becoming increasingly anxious about the prospects for launching a new round of multilateral trade talks. There was U.S. dissatisfaction over world trading practices (now included in the new areas of the Uruguay Round). Following the failure of the 1982 GATT ministerial meeting to get the round started, the United States began to search for alternative trade strategies, one of those being the FTA. This was meant to put pressure on the major trading countries of the world to refocus on the multilateral system.

Second, at the same time, the United States saw the FTA as a cautionary beacon for those involved in the GATT talks. If the talks failed, the FTA would be a precedent for other bilateral, or trilateral, trading deals. In case the world sundered into regional trading blocs, the FTA would at least preserve free trade between the two countries. Further, the FTA would provide an example of how the GATT could deal with some of the problematic issues that it faced. The FTA would be testimony that trade liberalization was still alive—even if not altogether well—worldwide. The FTA would show that even in the strained trading relations of the time, countries could still agree on clear, mutually advantageous and, in many cases, binding rules governing their trade and investment practices.

EC 1992

The move to full economic integration in the European Community by 1992 is coincidental to the FTA and not a planned reaction to it. The events surrounding the desire to achieve a single market are related to events internal to the Community that are unlike those of the FTA, which were largely external to the two participants. The motivations of the Community are related to the historical objective of "completing the internal market" and, importantly, to the recognition that the current situation perpetuates substantial trade impediments to achieving trade liberalization and the benefits derived from it.

The Pacific Rim

No discussion of regional trading blocs can be complete without reference to the increasing economic cooperation in some of the countries in the Asian Pacific region. Some observers remain skeptical about the possibility of regional trade liberalization in this region because of the enormous diversity in political and institutional factors. We, however, are not so quick to discount the possibility.

There are already indications that the Asian Pacific region is not going to remain passive in the current trading environment. Japan has now taken initiatives to increase economic cooperation in the region through some liberalization of trade in goods and investment flows, especially with the NIEs and the members of the Association of Southeast Asian Nations. There have also been discussions between Japan, ASEAN and Australia to review the potential for enhanced economic linkages. In addition, Australia and New Zealand have begun serious inquiries into the feasibility of a trilateral arrangement with Canada, which might later be extended to include the United States.[16]

What all this means for the world trading system is yet to be thought out or worked out. But it does seem clear that trade liberalization among the countries of the Pacific Rim will have consequences for world trade patterns and trade volumes and for the multilateral trading system.

The Benefits of Bilateralism

To understand and interpret the trend toward regional trading blocs, it is important to appreciate the benefits of integration. Because we have extensively studied the FTA, it is used here as a case in point.

At the outset, it should be recognized that accepting the FTA does not mean that Canada or the United States should place less importance on the GATT. On the contrary, an effective trade policy, especially for Canada, must rely on both the FTA and the multilateral trading system. The FTA gives Canada preferential access to its largest export market; the GATT offers significant gains in access to the markets of other countries. Each offers gains that the other cannot provide. For example, the FTA contains important trade-liberalizing measures in agriculture, but only through the GATT can crucial reforms of trade-distorting subsidies be effectively achieved. Similarly, greater multilateral liberalization in procurement can open up many more opportunities to both Canada and the United States than those accessed through the FTA.

However, it is also true that both countries were able to make gains through bilateral negotiations that could not realistically be achieved through multilateral negotiations, no matter how successful they prove to be. To demonstrate the point, consider some of the provisions contained in the FTA:[17]

- it offers the complete elimination of all tariffs, while the Uruguay Round calls for across-the-board cuts of about 35 percent;
- it eliminates many nontariff barriers that have proved difficult to contain through the GATT;
- it includes trade in many services and certainly with a greater degree of coverage than could be achieved through the GATT, where concessions must be balanced among all the major bargaining parties;
- it has dealt with specific trade disputes, such as the auto pact;
- it includes trade-related investment rules; and
- it creates a novel set of binational institutions to deal with trade disputes in general and countervail and antidumping cases in particular, and a commitment to develop a binational set of trade remedy laws.

Can anyone seriously argue that these provisions could be obtained through multilateral negotiations? We think not. The advantage of comprehensive bilateral agreements is that a gain in one sector can be balanced against a loss in another so that a net gain can be achieved by both parties.

IMPLICATIONS AND OPTIONS

This final section outlines the implications of the FTA for the trend toward regional trade liberalization. The fundamental issue addressed is whether the FTA should be taken as a harbinger of other trading blocs. A comment follows on how North America should view the trend or the possible emergence of a system of trading blocs.

The Raisons d'etre for Other Trading Blocs

The purpose of the discussion above on the genesis of the FTA was to highlight the underlying motivations that brought it about. What should be recognized is that although a mutually beneficial outcome was obtained—comprehensive bilateral trade liberalization—the initial objectives for contemplating and pursuing the agreement were different in each country. Similarly, strident moves toward complete economic integration in the EC were unrelated to the events occurring in North America. The point is that the raisons d'etre for regional trade agreements are as diverse as the countries that pursue them.

Consider some of the more obvious reasons for wanting to liberalize trade regionally.

Economic. As is the case for Canada under the FTA and for Australia and New Zealand through the Closer Economic Relationship, the desire to increase international competitiveness by producing for a larger market can be a prime motivation. Countries such as Canada, Australia and New Zealand have small domestic markets that inhibit the full realization of the scale economies that can be achieved through longer production runs and greater specialization. Thus, gaining expanded and secure access to a larger market is a prerequisite for such economies of scale to be a possibility.

Political. As noted, the driving force behind the U.S. moves to support Canada's trade initiative lay in the desires to pressure the major trading nations into launching a new GATT round and to demonstrate U.S. dissatisfaction over the current GATT status. In addition, there were domestic political pressures to quell the perceptions of U.S. trading partners that the United States was protectionist. The U.S.-Israel trade agreement and U.S. negotiations with the Caribbean basin nations also seem to have been politically motivated. Thus, political expediency can be, and usually is, of prime importance.

Strategic. It is hard to make a clear distinction between strategic, political and economic behavior. They are related, but "strategic" behavior is a useful categorization in the present context. We should divide this category further into aggressive, defensive and precautionary behavior.

The aggressive motivation for regional trade liberalization can be thought of as a beggar-thy-neighbor policy or fortress trading bloc. It would require the trading partners to look inward and would increase trade restrictions on the world outside the bloc. Some observers have argued that the FTA and EC 1992 have this motivation. We disagree since the FTA is GATT-consistent, complying with GATT Article XXIV, and there are no indications as yet that the Community will become more protectionist.

The defensive motive can be described simply as a reaction to the formation of other blocs. It is based on the premise that any move toward regional trade liberalization is necessarily aggressive and thus creates the desire to secure access to a large market. The current initiative by New Zealand to have free trade with Canada and Australia might be thought of in this light.

The precautionary motive, or hedge, is based on the presumption that the world trading system might fail. In other words, this motivation presents an alternative if the GATT fails to achieve further multilateral trade liberalization or maintain the current level. The nature of U.S. involvement in the early FTA negotiations can be seen in this light. This is dangerous from the point of view of the world trading system because the proliferation of trading blocs as a hedge against the failure of the GATT could lead to a self-fulfilling prophecy.

The FTA: Leader of the Pack?

The relevant question then is: does the Free Trade Agreement provide a necessary and sufficient condition for other countries to initiate regional groupings? To answer this question, let us look back at the motives outlined above.

Economic. The desire to achieve international competitiveness by producing for a larger market need not be fulfilled only through regional arrangements. Indeed, the widest possible access for domestic exporters to foreign markets can best be achieved through the GATT. However, as is the case for the FTA, certain gains can best be achieved through bilateralism. The FTA can be seen as a model for those pursuing these types of gains. But the FTA only demonstrates what has been known for years—a comprehensive regional trading agreement can be mutually beneficial, even if countries are of different size and economic strength, because gains and losses can better balance out. Therefore, North America lags rather than leads the pack in providing an economic rationale for regional groupings.

Political. There is no clear reason why politicians in other countries should react to the FTA by sounding calls for their own regional trading arrangements. After all, political expediency supported the Canada-U.S. trade initiative on one side of the border but not the other.

Strategic. Unless the FTA incites a trade war, there is no reason why it should prompt aggressive reactions from the countries' trading partners. It might, however, lead to defensive and precautionary reactions that may induce regional groupings. Although there are many possible outcomes to consider, we present three.

First, even if the FTA is GATT-consistent and neutral in the sense that it does nothing to increase trade restrictions in third countries, it can still be welfare-reducing to those countries. While rationalization may take place and the volume of trade may grow within the bloc, there may also be trade diversion. This might be a problem, for example, for small countries like New Zealand and Australia that compete with the United States in the Canadian agricultural market and that face the potential of a significant loss in trade. These countries might then seek out areas of security of access through bilateral or plurilateral arrangements.

Second, consider the effect on the world trading system if the FTA turns both Canada and the United States inward. This might be the case, for example, if Canadian negotiators pressured the United States in the GATT talks to maintain trade barriers imposed on third countries. This pressure may arise because any multilateral reduction in trade barriers will erode the Canadian preferential treatment that the FTA affords in the U.S. market. If this were to happen, it could reduce U.S. support for the GATT, a result that would threaten multilateralism and stimulate regionalism.

Third, the United States may opt for negotiating more bilateral free trade agreements, or third countries might accede to the FTA. In this case, the U.S. would be seen as directly responsible for promoting regional trading blocs. Any such U.S. action would certainly create strains in the world trading system and would prompt calls for defensive trade policy options.

What can be concluded from all of the above? Is the U.S.-Canada FTA a harbinger of regional trading blocs? There is no single compelling reason to think that it is contributing to this development. We are attracted to the argument of Lipsey and Smith that relies partly on the premise that the economic size of the whole (i.e., the combined U.S. and Canadian market) is only 10 percent greater than the size of the largest part, and partly on the natural affinities and trade relations that the two countries share.[18] Also, the underlying motivations are not likely due to the desire to exploit mutual gains or to exert commercial power. Smith adds that free trade areas are also outward looking.[19]

However, there is a note of caution. One cannot completely dismiss the demonstration effect the U.S.-Canada FTA assuredly has on the rest of the world. Although it clearly does not suggest that the world should aggressively adopt regional trading blocs, it does re-assert the benefits of bilateralism.

TRADE POLICY OPTIONS

How then should North America view the trend toward, or the possible emergence of, a system of regional trading blocs? The answer to this question is straightforward. Since the GATT's inception in 1947, the multilateral trading system has served its members well by promoting a dramatic increase in the volume of world trade. A system of regional trading blocs could serve its participants well; however, the system of preferences could also reduce world trade and welfare. In addition, it could reduce the political commitment and economic interest in the Uruguay Round of the GATT. Thus, our answer to this question is that North America should view such a trend with disapproval.

This leads us to consider what the trade policy options are for North America. Ostry outlines three key options for dealing with the current trading system:[20]

(1) muddle through the current GATT round and otherwise maintain a "business as usual" approach;
(2) accept that the "GATT is dead," as Lester Thurow of MIT has asserted, and opt for a triad-based system of managed trade; or
(3) strengthen the GATT and vigorously pursue multilateralism.

Option #1 is risky and not satisfactory in the world we have described above. We therefore exclude it.

Option #2 is also a tenuous road to travel and full of pitfalls. Managed trade in the triad—Japan, the United States and Europe—could incite retaliation, and it requires leadership and commitment in the United States that would not likely be forthcoming. It also does not reflect the realities of an increasingly globalized and technologically changing world and, importantly, would exclude a large part of world trade. For these and other reasons, this can be rejected as a sensible option.

Option #3 is thus left—a renewed and vigorous approach to the Uruguay and subsequent Rounds of the GATT.

A successful set of negotiations can result in a substantial liberalization of trade and in the extension of coverage to the "new" areas and can effect a strengthening of the GATT as an institution. It would also radically diminish the system of preferences that a group of regional trading blocs could provide. In a world with this outcome, the impetus for future bilateralism or regional groupings could be reduced.

NOTES

1. Paul R. Krugman and Maurice Obstfeld, *International Economics: Theory and Policy* (Glenview, Ill.: Scott, Foresman and Company, 1988); and Martin Feldstein and Charles Horioka, "Domestic Saving and International Capital Flows," *Economic Journal* (June 1985).
2. George Hatsopoulos, Paul Krugman and Lawrence Summers, "Competitiveness: Beyond the Trade Deficit," a paper presented to the Canadian-American Committee (Boston, March 1989).
3. Bruce R. Scott, "National Strategies: Key to International Competition," in *U.S. Competitiveness in the World Economy*, ed. Bruce R. Scott and George C. Lodge (Boston: Harvard Business School Press, 1985).
4. A good reference to the Industrial Policy School literature is Richard G. Lipsey and Wendy Dobson, eds., *Shaping Comparative Advantage* (Toronto, Ont.: C.D. Howe Institute, 1987).
5. See Paul R. Krugman, ed., *Strategic Trade Policy and the New International Economics* (Cambridge, Mass.: MIT Press, 1986).

6. This is nothing more than a verbal description of the Prisoner's Dilemma, where a Nash-equilibrium is represented by noncooperation and defensive trade policies and where a pareto optimal outcome is trade liberalization.
7. The term globalization was originally defined by Professor Theodore Levitt of the Harvard Business School.
8. John F. Helliwell, "From Now Till Then: Globalization and Economic Cooperation," *Canadian Public Policy*, XV Supplement (February 1989), p. 571.
9. Ibid., p. 74.
10. Ibid., p. 76.
11. This is the view, for example, of former U.S. Treasury Secretary James Baker in "The Geopolitical Implications of the U.S.-Canada Trade Pact," *The International Economy* (January/February 1988).
12. Sylvia Ostry, "Global Trends: Global Solutions," notes of an address to Queen's University, School of Policy Studies, Inaugural Conference, 1989, p. 18.
13. Ibid., and Murray G. Smith, "Canada's Stake in the Uruguay Round and the GATT System," mimeo (Ottawa, Ont.: Institute for Research on Public Policy, 1989).
14. James Baker, when he was U.S. Treasury Secretary, stated that the Reagan Administration had defended U.S. interests by imposing more protection than any Administration in the past 50 years. See Baker, "Remarks before a Conference at the Institute for International Economics" (September 14, 1987).
15. Simon Reisman, "Canada-United States Free Trade," in *The Issue of Free Trade in U.S.-Canadian Relations: Next Step?* ed. Earl Fried and Paul Triziese (Washington, D.C.: Brookings Institution, 1984).
16. Frank Holmes, Ralph Lattimore and Anthony Haas, *Partners in the Pacific* (Wellington, New Zealand: Trade Development Board, 1988).
17. This material draws heavily upon Boxes 1, 2 and 3 in Richard G. Lipsey and Robert C. York, *Evaluating the Free Trade Deal: A Guided Tour through the Canada-U.S. Agreement* (Toronto, Ont.: C.D. Howe Institute, 1988).
18. Richard G. Lipsey and Murray S. Smith, "Canada-U.S. FTA: Special Case or Wave of the Future," in *Free Trade Areas and U.S. Trade Policy*, ed. Jeffrey J. Schott (Washington, D.C.: Institute for International Economics, 1989).
19. Murray G. Smith, "What Is at Stake," in *Bilateralism, Multilateralism and Canada in U.S. Trade Policy*, ed. William Diebold, Jr. (Cambridge, Mass.: Ballinger Publishing Co., 1988).
20. The following draws upon Ostry, "Global Trends."

Asian Responses to the Growth of Trading Blocs

9

by Dick K. Nanto

Many policymakers are concerned about the Asian response to the growth of regional trading blocs. There is no one Asian response, of course, just as there is no one Latin American or African response to these blocs. The diverse Asian Pacific region represents an amalgamation of nations and part nations at different levels of development and with distinct histories and cultures. The "Asian responses" focused on in this chapter include those of Japan and its neighbors in East Asia.

DEVELOPING HORIZONTAL RELATIONSHIPS

Despite the differences within the region, a new pattern of horizontal integration is emerging among the economies of Japan, South Korea, Taiwan, Hong Kong, Singapore, Thailand, and Indonesia. Fostering this change in trade and investment flows is the strong export performance of these East Asian countries combined with the appreciation of the yen and the threat of increased protectionism in American and European markets.

The United States traditionally has been the main market for Asian exporters rather than other countries in the region. While this trend is continuing, Japan is increasingly becoming a major export market for the newly industrializing economies of Asia, particularly South Korea and Taiwan. Exports to Japan from the Asian NIEs have been growing at rates exceeding 30 percent in recent years, with Japan now taking about 13 percent of their exports, almost double the 1985 rate of 7 percent. Furthermore, in 1988, Japan's imports of industrial goods from the Association of Southeast Asian Nations jumped by 50 percent. (ASEAN includes Indonesia, Malaysia, Singapore, Thailand, Brunei, and the Philippines.)

In addition, more direct investment is flowing from Japan into the Asian NIEs. Japanese investment in other countries in Asia rose from $1.4 billion in 1985 to $4.8 billion in 1987. However, that level of investment is still small compared with Japan's $15 billion level of direct investment in the United States in 1988.

Much of this change in investment flows can be attributed to the strong yen. Japan is being forced to move out of labor-intensive industries because of rising imports from countries with lower wage rates and workers who can be trained to perform relatively skill-intensive tasks.

Another important factor is market liberalization in Japan, fostered to a great extent by U.S. pressures. With the opening of Japan's markets, imports have flowed in not only from the United States but also from a number of other countries. As Japan has liberalized its market for steel, for example, South Korea has jumped in, as has Taiwan. Similarly, Japan has entered South Korea's liberalized market for consumer goods. Trade among the economies of the Asian Pacific is, in fact, growing faster than their trade with countries outside the region.

In providing the impetus for market liberalization, the United States plays the role of villain, while Japan reaps many of the benefits and can claim to champion the rights of the Asian developing nations. At the Montreal Summit in 1988, for instance, Japan tried to stake a claim as the voice of the NIEs in Asia.

Also significant in altering the trade and investment pattern in Asia is the emergence of the so-called Japan-NIEs—the newly industrializing Asian economies in which the Japanese have established manufacturing plants that have begun to export back to Japan. Many of the products, originally designed to sell locally or in the United States, carry Japanese brand names and are well suited to Japanese tastes. A 1987 survey by Japan's trade ministry indicated that about 15 percent of the output of Japanese manufacturing facilities in Asia is shipped back to Japan. About 50 percent of the electrical appliances imported into Japan are produced by subsidiaries of Japanese companies. The sudden rise from almost zero to over 50 percent in the import share of the Japanese market for 35mm cameras, for example, can be traced to Japan-NIEs. The imported cameras are not made by Kodak or Leica but by Canon or Minolta and are assembled in manufacturing subsidiaries in Singapore and other countries.

Japan's changing product demands have helped to shape the new trade pattern. Japan's previous emphasis primarily on food and raw material imports is shifting toward manufactured goods. In 1983, Japan imported nearly twice as much in mineral fuels as in manufactured goods; by 1987, the reverse was occurring. Manufactured goods are currently about 44 percent of Japanese imports.

As long as Japan concentrated its imports on needed food and raw materials, the NIEs with developing manufacturing bases could find only small markets in Japan compared with those in the United States. Countries such as Indonesia and Canada with energy, ore or wheat to export could run a surplus in their balance of trade with Japan. Countries without such exports had a trade deficit with Japan and usually countered that imbalance by running a surplus with the United States. This situation is now changing.

The Asian Pacific countries recognize their growing economic clout and their strengthening intraregional trade. At the same time, however, they do not intend to jeopardize their existing trading relationships, particularly with the United States, by forming an exclusive regional trading bloc.

Because the United States remains the top export market for most Asian NIEs and Japan, the nightmare of these countries is being shut out of North American markets. They are thus pursuing initiatives to ensure they are locked into growing regional trading blocs, especially in North America and Europe. Proposed strategies include a free trade agreement (FTA) between the United States and Japan similar to the Canada-U.S. accord and a Pacific Rim organization to coordinate economic policies and facilitate cooperation on issues of mutual interest.

U.S. PROPOSALS

The proposals being considered in the United States for an Asian FTA or a Pacific organization are numerous and varied. These proposals are still preliminary, although some legislation has been introduced in the 101st Congress.

Sen. Max Baucus has introduced a bill that would initiate trade negotiations with Japan for the purpose of increasing economic coordination between the United States and Japan through one or more agreements. The aim is to eliminate any current account imbalance between the two countries, liberalize trade and improve dispute settlement procedures, and better allocate the strategic burden between the two countries.

Rep. Philip Crane has introduced bills to establish FTAs between the United States and Japan, Taiwan, South Korea, or ASEAN.

Sen. Bill Bradley has proposed a coalition of eight Pacific nations to coordinate exchange rates, seek solutions to the Third World debt crisis, and negotiate common positions for the GATT talks. The so-called Pac-8 would include the industrialized countries of the United States, Canada, Japan, and Australia and the NIEs of Mexico, South Korea and two from ASEAN.

Sen. Alan Cranston and Rep. Mel Levine have introduced bills calling for a Pacific Basin forum to discuss economic, diplomatic and other issues unique to the region.

Sen. William Roth has expressed interest in a U.S.-Taiwan free trade area. A report from the Congressional Research Service examines this issue.[1]

At the request of Sen. Lloyd Bentsen, the International Trade Commission has recently released two reports examining the pros and cons of free trade areas. The first deals with the possibility of initiating negotiations to establish an FTA with Japan; the second looks at possible FTAs with Korea, Taiwan and ASEAN.[2]

Despite the large number of bills that propose an FTA with Japan or other countries in Asia, passage of such a bill within the next few years is remote. The focus of U.S. policy is on completing the Uruguay Round of the GATT negotiations. Also impeding development of a U.S.-Asian FTA at this time is considerable trade friction between U.S. and Asian exporters, different levels of development, probable protectionist backlash from unrestricted Asian imports, and wide cultural gaps. However, the United States will likely continue to strengthen the institutions in the Pacific that deal with coordination and cooperation; those that involve lowering trade barriers can be strengthened without establishing an FTA.

The most probable future FTAs for the United States are with Mexico and possibly with the Caribbean nations. The United States might also approach the European Community to establish a customs union or other arrangement to lower trade barriers. The U.S. might then consider an FTA with the economies of Asia.

The greatest political pressures in the United States for a U.S.-Asian FTA would likely originate from conservatives interested in negotiating an agreement with Taiwan (given its increasing diplomatic isolation in the world) and from groups concerned with deteriorating relations between the U.S. and Japan. The greatest political pressures against such an FTA would likely come from U.S. labor, American businesses competing with low cost imports from Asia, and U.S. industries such as textiles, steel and automobiles whose products are currently protected from imports.

BASIC TRADE PROBLEMS FOR JAPAN AND THE ASIAN NIEs

Friction with the United States continues to be a major trade concern for all the East Asians. They are particularly concerned about the Super 301 provisions in the 1988 Omnibus Trade and Competitiveness Act and the very likely possibility that each may some day be named a priority country practicing unfair trade practices. Japan, Korea, Taiwan, and other Asian exporters lobbied to keep off this list of countries, although Japan did not succeed. Certain members of Congress have argued that the original purpose of Super 301 was to designate the Asian nations, especially Japan, as unfair traders; many in Congress had made it clear they would be displeased should Japan be omitted from the list.[3] (In fact, Japan might be better off now targeted under Super 301 than if it had not been listed and thus had been at the center of the political storm that probably would have erupted.[4])

Trade friction with the United States will also intensify due to the apparent intent of the Bush Administration to continue the aggressive trade policies that characterized Reagan's last three years in the White House. Given this prospect, Japan and the other Asian nations should attempt to resolve trade differences in a less political manner. The constant wrangling has created much ill will not only in the United States but around the world and is one reason that an FTA or similar framework is being looked to as an alternative to current methods of solving trade problems.

In addition to trade friction with the United States, a major problem for the East Asian NIEs is their trade deficit with Japan. For example, South Korea, distressed over its chronic trade deficit with Japan, has begun a program to diversify imports from Japan to the United States. It has gone so far as to compile a list of its current Japanese imports and to designate alternative Korean or American suppliers.[5] Taiwan is following a buy-American policy in its public procurement, although it recently scaled back the program's public construction projects.

Even though the NIEs are frustrated with their trade relations with Japan and say they do not want to buy from Japan, their businesses continue to do so. Japanese products are competitively priced, and Japanese exporters typically provide the desired after-market service. Thus, while increased trade with Japan has brought some undesirable consequences, dependence on Japan seems to be growing.

An example of structural dependence on Japan can be seen in the relationship between the Samsung Company in South Korea and the TDK company in Japan. TDK is the only supplier of a critical silicon rubber seal used by Samsung and other Korean manufacturers in microwave ovens assembled in Korea. Indeed, to determine how many ovens are made by Korean assemblers, one need only find out how many seals TDK has shipped to Korea. Further, Japan could destroy this segment of the microwave industry by cutting off the shipments of door seals to Korea.[6]

Other Asian economies show similar dependence on Japanese machinery, components and capital. However, this import dependence has also helped the Asian NIEs to export to Japan. In Thailand, the Japanese private sector has assisted Thai businesses in upgrading the quality of their exports. A boom in Thai exports of food and light manufactures to Japan has helped erode the long-standing Thai perception that Japan's markets are closed. Japan is the largest foreign investor in Thailand, and reportedly no Thai-Japan joint venture has ever failed.

ASIAN REGIONAL COOPERATION: A DE FACTO BLOC

As noted above, the probability of a formal Asian Pacific trading bloc, particularly one that excludes the United States, is small. Most of the Asian Pacific nations are committed to the multilateral GATT liberalization process rather than to a plurilateral trading bloc arrangement. If the East Asian NIEs were to join a trading bloc, they are seemingly more interested in an arrangement with the United States than with Japan. They rely heavily on the American market for export sales and share important security and other ties with the United States.

Also impeding formation of an Asian bloc is the aversion of the Asian nations that were victims of Japanese aggression in World War II to a regional trading bloc dominated by Japan. Even though the proportion of the population directly affected by the war is decreasing throughout Asia, considerable hostility continues to dog Japan's efforts to erase the lingering memories of its World War II atrocities and its attempt to establish the Greater East Asia Co-Prosperity Sphere. This hostility surfaces when, for example, Japan rewrites its history books to downplay historical Japanese aggression in China. Although Japan needs to settle the issue permanently, the problem is unlikely to be resolved soon given the current instability in Japan's Liberal Democratic Party.

Another reason that a formal Asian bloc is unlikely at this time is the NIEs' trade deficit with Japan, discussed above.

Despite these problems, however, the Asian Pacific nations are bolstering formal ties and cooperative relations among themselves. In Japan, the Ministry of International Trade and Industry has organized an annual conference of trade and industry ministers from "core" Asian Pacific nations (and including the United States) to concentrate on trade and investment issues. Japan's Ministry of Foreign Affairs supports the 15-member Pacific Economic Cooperation Conference, established in September 1980, that is increasingly being viewed as the nucleus of a Pacific economic organization. The conference is expanding its role in the region and in 1989 began publishing an economic outlook for the Pacific area similar to that issued by the Organization for Economic Cooperation and Development.

Australian Prime Minister Robert Hawke has proposed the establishment of a more formal Asian Pacific economic organization that would include a permanent secretariat for core nations and would be modeled after the OECD. This organization would not constitute a regional trading bloc but would boost the GATT liberalization process. The first ministerial conference of this group, which adopted the name of APEC (Asia Pacific Economic Cooperation), met in November 1989 in Canberra. The 12 nations attending agreed that the region should work toward greater economic cooperation, particularly in multilateral trade reform, but disagreed on whether APEC should be formalized as an institution. There was virtually no support for the idea of forming a trading bloc based on preferential tariff rates.

Whether a formal Asian Pacific bloc is created or not is, in fact, largely immaterial because a de facto trading bloc is emerging. It is arising out of economic necessity and will continue to grow regardless of the development of a formal free trade agreement among the various economies. Japan's business executives do not need free trade to operate. They are skillful at working around trade barriers, having dealt with their own Ministry of International Trade and Industry for decades.

Furthermore, the idea of unrestricted imports from Asian neighbors appears contrary to current Japanese government behavior. Although Japan provides special tariff preferences for Asian and less developed country exporters to its market, it also intervenes to protect Japanese industries from too rapid incursions of imports. Japan pressured South Korea to control its exports of cement and certain textiles, for example, and asked Indonesia to restrain its exports of plywood (although Indonesia refused).

JAPAN'S RESPONSE TO EC INTEGRATION

Japan has been watching the unfolding drama of the European Community's planned economic integration by 1992 with interest and apprehension. The Japanese are fascinated with the change in attitude within the EC, from the "Europessimism" prevalent during the early 1980s to the optimism and confidence that EC 1992 has brought. However, Japan is worried that it could be left out as the EC economy surges forward. Specific concerns center on four issues: increased protectionism, domestic content requirements for Japanese manufacturing subsidiaries, reciprocity, and proposed retaliation for infringement of intellectual property rights.[7]

Japan lives by trading and hence fears a "Fortress Europe" emerging from EC 1992. The Japanese see the highly protectionist measures already taken by individual member countries as spreading to the community as a whole. Ten EC nations currently impose quantitative restrictions on 89 Japanese products, including Spain with 41 and France with 17. How much access will be given to Japan's exports of automobiles, for example, in view of the rigid French and Italian import quotas on Japanese passenger cars and Japan's voluntary restriction of 1.25 million autos to be exported to the EC in 1989?

In addition, the EC has taken rapid action against what it considers to be Japan's "laser-beam" exports (targeting specific narrow sectors for rapid export penetration) by imposing antidumping duties, asking for voluntary restraints or smothering the imports in red tape.[8]

Japan's concerns about European content requirements stem from the EC's so-called screwdriver plant policies. These are designed to thwart Japanese exporters' attempts to circumvent antidumping duties by establishing assembly plants within the Community that require little more than final assembly (by screwdriver) of parts shipped from Japan. The EC generally requires 40 percent local content for products to qualify as European in origin, but the level for video cassette recorders is 45 percent and for automobiles as high as 80 percent.

Reciprocity in financial services and government procurement along with retaliation for infringement of intellectual property rights seem aimed particularly at Japan and the Asian NIEs. Both concepts appear to threaten unilateral action by the EC.

RETHINKING STATUS AND ROLES

The emerging European and North American trading blocs have nudged Asian strategic thinkers toward their own backyards. In a sense, EC integration and the U.S.-Canada FTA have provided a unique opportunity for Japan to gain leadership in Asia at the expense of the Western industrial powers and for the Asian NIEs to rethink their heavy dependence on the United States.

Japan currently is in an ideal economic position to wield more influence among its neighbors in Asia. With a GNP second only to the United States and a per capita income level exceeding that of Americans, Japan can channel its credit, foreign aid, trade, and overseas investment in a manner that will enhance its power and influence in the region. So many nations attended the funeral of Emperor Hirohito probably not because of great admiration for a reclusive monarch whose role in Japan's aggression in Asia is still debated. Rather, their attendance more likely reflected the recognition around the world of the powerful economic status that Japan has attained.

Japan can now call some of the shots in world economic affairs. It is rising in power in international organizations such as the International Monetary Fund, and it must become a key player in resolving global issues such as Third World debt and currency alignment.

Japan is confident that it can generally deal with protectionism as long as Japanese exporters are competitive. Most border trade barriers are in fact quite low among the industrialized countries. Average tariff rates are far below the levels of the 1930s when trading blocs threatened Japanese security. The advantages provided to U.S. and Canadian firms under the Free Trade Agreement actually are small compared with fluctuations in exchange rates; few formal barriers can compare with the 50 percent appreciation of the yen.

In sum, although Japan and the Asian NIEs will likely continue to view the growing trading blocs in Europe and North America with concern, they are unlikely to take drastic countermeasures such as forming a bloc of their own. They see existing blocs as somewhat defensive actions against their exports and are confident they can work within those environments, especially if direct foreign investments are not prohibited.

The Asian Pacific economic powers will continue to monitor policymaking in current blocs and to object to provisions inimical to their interests. They will push to extend their links with the United States, probably more through extensive economic cooperation than through a formal FTA. They will also likely step up diplomatic efforts with neighboring nations to discuss economic policy and pursue matters of mutual interest.

The opinions expressed are the author's and not necessarily those of the Congressional Research Service or the U.S. government.

NOTES

1. William H. Cooper, *Taiwan-U.S. Free Trade Area: Economic Effects and Related Issues*, Report No. 89-96 E (Washington, D.C.: Congressional Research Service, U.S. Library of Congress, 1989).
2. U.S. International Trade Commission, *Pros and Cons of Initiating Negotiations with Japan to Explore the Possibility of a U.S.-Japan Free Trade Area Agreement*, USITC Pub. 2120 (Washington, D.C., 1989); and *The Pros and Cons of Entering into Negotiations on Free Trade Area Agreements with Taiwan, the Republic of Korea, and ASEAN, or the Pacific Rim in General*, USITC Pub. 2166 (Washington, D.C., 1989).
3. Keith M. Rockwell, "Congress Wants Japan on Unfair Trade List," *Journal of Commerce*, May 1, 1989, p. 1A.
4. Bill Arbruster, "Trade Talk," *The Washington Post*, March 30, 1989, p. 5A.
5. Dick K. Nanto, *Japan-South Korea Economic Relations: South Korea's Approach to the "Japan Problem,"* Report No. 87-953 E (Washington, D.C.: Congressional Research Service, 1987), pp. 18-21.
6. Woong Suh Park, Executive Vice President, Samsung Co., in a private interview with the author in Seoul, Korea, June 5, 1987.
7. "The External Implications of the Single European Market: A View From Japan," statement by Michihiko Kunihiro, Deputy Minister for Foreign Affairs, given at the Royal Institute of International Affairs, October 11, 1988.
8. Dick K. Nanto, *European Community-Japan Trade Relations: A European Perspective*, Report No. 86-166 E (Washington, D.C.: Congressional Research Service, 1986), pp. 11-29.

Seizing the Opportunity Presented by LDC Blocs

10

by Richard Tropp

THE REFLEXIVE POLICY CATECHISM

Several years ago, an African finance minister spent an entire evening telling me of his hopes for the regional trading bloc in his area. He believed the establishment of this bloc would encourage firms in his country to reach out to regional markets, to be forced beyond business strategies of protection through import substitution. Export-oriented policies would be needed to compete with businesses in the surrounding six or eight countries, he said. The agreement would compel his country's protected firms to compete with other firms beyond their borders in the region and would eventually make firms in his nation better able to compete in the general world market.

Catching his enthusiasm, I related the discussion to my boss at the Agency for International Development. As members of the Reagan Administration, we eschewed the ideology behind regional trading blocs, holding that blocs inhibit international competition and hurt business. But I emphasized that blocs already exist and that many developing country finance ministers and firms depend on them to expand markets for business in their countries. I proposed that the U.S. government try to help those countries use the regional blocs rationally. My boss's initial reaction was positive. However, he returned the next day from a meeting with senior officials of the State Department in which the idea had been discussed and told me that it was my worst idea in four years. He reiterated the economists' traditional catechism for why regional trading blocs do not work and will therefore disappear over the long term.

During my government tenure, the United States consistently maintained its opposition to regional trading blocs, a position it continues to uphold in theory, even though blocs are a reality to the businesses in the less developed countries (LDCs). The government has ignored organizations such as the Latin American Free Trade Association (LAFTA), the Andean Pact, the Economic Community of West Africa, and the Southern African Development Conference on the grounds that economic theory suggests they lead to higher transaction costs but no greater aggregate number of transactions. The government has opposed blocs in Europe and Asia on the grounds that they are harmful to member countries, that blocs engage in what economists call trade diversion rather than trade creation (or "substitution" rather than "additionality," as the development community puts it). The U.S. government believes blocs inhibit businesses in bloc countries from reaching beyond their nations' borders into the world trading system.

In fact, the United States has attacked the economic legitimacy of Third World regional trading blocs at every possible opportunity of which I am aware in the past eight years. It has argued that blocs contravene the GATT system and that bloc member countries fundamentally oppose a multilateral trading system and are moving in a fundamentally different direction in trade policy from where most of the world wants to go.

Further, the U.S. government and U.S. business view developing country agreements with the European Community as constraints or barriers to free trade. Most Americans in business appear to argue not from trade or economic theory but from generalizations based on individual experiences, which have led them to perceive such agreements as harmful to their businesses. In turn, the U.S. government—i.e., the Office of the U.S. Trade Representative and the Commerce Department—has tended to defend U.S. business against what it views as a threat.

Nevertheless, despite U.S. opposition and economic theory, regional trading blocs are a fact. The LDCs strongly believe in them. Moreover, I believe these trading agreements present opportunities for, not barriers to, U.S. business.

BY CONTRAST, LDC REALITIES

The underlying economic condition in the LDCs is that most businesses cannot sell products internationally because they do not know how to produce anything that will meet world market standards. LDC governments feel that if they are required to open their borders and to allow their businesses to compete in the global economy, their people will very quickly go out of business.

In terms of the viewpoint of LDC governments and businesses toward regional blocs, they are concerned about being overwhelmed by America, Europe or Japan, but they are not focusing on shutting these nations out of their home markets. In fact, it is far more likely that the LDCs are not thinking about them at all; instead, the LDCs are trying to adjust to the change from competing only in a domestic market protected by import substitution policies to competing within a broader market of neighboring developing countries.

Their policies are not designed to respond to U.S. policies or to change GATT mechanisms; we are not even on their radar screens. When, say, Ecuador thinks about the opportunities and risks of regional trading blocs, it thinks about Brazil and Argentina as competitive threats that could overwhelm it. When Honduras contemplates these opportunities and risks, it thinks about Guatemala, which is the advanced economy of Central America, or about El Salvador. When Mali thinks about regional trading blocs, which it often does, it sees opportunities for its businesses to enter Nigeria's market and the possibility that the Nigerians will be better able to compete in Mali. When Bangladesh thinks about regional trading blocs, it obviously thinks about India.

Thus, the first reality from the LDCs' point of view—which we must understand—is that the United States is not part of their reality. Their businesses do not expect that they will ever be competitive with U.S. businesses, either in the U.S. market or in their home markets. They do not view their regional trading blocs as a means either to shut out the United States or to create opportunities for themselves here. Rather, they envision new markets and expansion within those countries that form their regional bloc.

AMERICAN VERSUS LDC PERCEPTIONS

From the U.S. business view, what opportunities and what risks are created when regional trading blocs are established by LDCs? How does the U.S. business view differ from that of an LDC business?

Before the establishment of the Andean Pact, for example, Ecuador could not export to Venezuela, Peru or Bolivia. Within the Andean Pact, even given all its constraints, Ecuador can pick the country that has the weakest barriers against its products, move in by establishing a joint venture with the government or a business, and then export from it into all the other countries around it.

What has happened is that the regional trading bloc has created an opening through the weakest part of the "sieve" into the whole bloc. This view is common among businesses in the LDC world, even though it is difficult for those in the U.S. to understand. In addition, to the extent that LDC businesses consider the United States at all, they believe that the formation of LDC blocs creates *openings* for the United States—the same openings they are creating for themselves.

Similarly, if one were to ask a European, "What do you think the effects of EC 1992 will be with respect to the United States?"

some of the more sophisticated would respond, "If the United States is smart, its businesses will realize that some former Spanish colonies will now accede to the Lomé Convention. The Lomé Convention countries, which are mostly African nations, can now export, for the most part, duty and quota free into Europe." This means that if one believes that Spain, as a condition of its accession, may require, say, the Dominican Republic to become part of the Lomé Convention, then a savvy U.S. business would be able to use the Dominican Republic as an export platform through Spain into the rest of Europe.

There is not one U.S. business out of 100 that envisions this type of opportunity arising from EC 1992, nor does the U.S. government see this as an opportunity. Europeans and Latins, however, do recognize the possibilities. They only wonder why Americans do not take advantage of them. From the Europeans' point of view, EC 1992 is an opening into what was previously a more closed system. The United States, on the other hand, sees the closing of what was previously a relatively more open system.

Thus, regional trading blocs can be an alternative—not to free trade, but to the existential reality of individual country walls and import substitution. For the most part, Latin, African and South Asian countries have erected walls to protect their businesses from outside competition, and those indigenous businesses' inefficient methods of production are, in effect, subsidized by that country's consumers. When these countries join a regional trading bloc, they remove protections that, say, Honduran businesses used to have from competition by more efficient Salvadoran or Guatemalan businesses.

The difference between LDC and U.S. viewpoints reminds one of the theological debate about the Biblical punishment, "an eye for an eye." From a Western point of view, this punishment seems fairly drastic. However, in Old Testament times, if someone chopped off a relative's limb or took out an eye, vengeance could entail marshaling one's whole tribe to hunt down and kill the offender. Then, one might kill everybody in the offender's immediate family, and perhaps a few cousins for good measure. Thus, "an eye for an eye" really was meant to *limit* the punishment that otherwise would have been imposed. Similarly, regional trading blocs limit the constraints imposed by what in their absence would have been the import substitution barriers of individual developing nations.

The countries that create these blocs and the businesses within a bloc understand this. Whereas they used to be protected, they are now subject to competition from the businesses of other bloc members, and they must really learn how to compete. This perception is, of course, entirely different from the U.S. view of the results of the establishment of regional trading blocs.

Trade Creation or Trade Diversion?

Do regional trading blocs cause trade creation or trade diversion or, as the development community would say, do blocs create additionality or (trade) substitution? In theory, regional trading blocs, as opposed to worldwide competition, might create substitution instead of additionality. In fact, however, almost all blocs in the LDCs have a type of clearinghouse arrangement. This arrangement encourages trade denominated in local currency rather than in hard currency. Once every six months or so, the books are cleared of hard currency balances.

Although this system may create a series of problems, from the point of view of local businesses or of U.S. corporations it creates a viable second currency—another vehicle through which they can trade. For those with access to dollars, this may not matter. But for businesses in, say, Honduras that could never gain access to dollars—either because the central bank did not have them or because the bureaucratic hassle of using influence and time to obtain them was too great—this suddenly presents an exciting new option.

LDC business people will often say, "Yesterday we could trade with another country only if we had dollars, which was essentially impossible. Today, we can trade with that country because the trading bloc has created another currency through which we can clear trades."

There are a number of developing countries where the central bank does have dollars. In fact, a particular trade transaction may be sufficiently beneficial to such a country that a rational central bank could be expected to allocate the dollars to it. But in the LDC real world, there are transfer costs to every such transaction. Perfect allocation of foreign exchange does not exist. Instead, there is a series of hurdles in which businesses have to engage the attention of civil servants, wait in long queues, complete extensive paperwork, and expose their books to uncomfortable outside examination in order to obtain dollars.

With the establishment of regional trading blocs, such hassles are reduced. Sometimes another series of hassles—usually not as onerous—is created. Hence, from a local LDC business point of view, blocs create a new medium of exchange and thus are certain to produce so-called additionality. To LDC businesses, these are great real-world benefits.

CONSTRAINTS TO THE POSITIVE IMPACT OF BLOCS

I have stressed so far the positive aspects of regional trading blocs as viewed by LDC businesses and LDC finance ministers.

However, in looking at the economic literature, the most obvious conclusion is that most regional agreements simply do not work in the long run, in the sense that they do not appear to increase trade with the world beyond the bloc.

The arrangement seems to work for a while *within* the trading bloc. There is a period during which the LDC businesses that had been protected by import substitution laws become more competitive. For example, Honduran businesses become able to compete with Guatemalan and Salvadoran businesses. This increase in competitiveness typically lasts for 10 to 20 years in the Central American common market, for about 10 years in the Economic Community of West Africa, and for 2 to 3 years in the Andean Pact. Then the benefits stop because the businesses have become as competitive as they are able to within the protected constraints of these regions.

Another development over time is that countries tend to build up imbalances versus each other. While El Salvador and Guatemala become net creditors, Honduras and Costa Rica become net debtors. After a while, Honduras and Costa Rica no longer like the arrangement, so they pull out formally or just stop trading within the bloc. This or a similar chronology of events has happened in virtually every LDC regional trading bloc around the world, except in the Economic Community of West Africa.

Another constraint is that political differences tend to surface over time. This is particularly evident in, for example, East Africa between Kenya, on the one hand, and Uganda and Tanzania, on the other. What used to be, or potentially was, a generally smoothly working regional economic system disintegrates as one of the governments steps in to reap political benefits and thus distorts the process. For instance, Kenya might press Uganda to use trucking instead of railroads for all its transportation, to help subsidize the Kenyan trucking industry.

Over time, therefore, LDC regional trading blocs seem to atrophy slowly. The research literature shows that blocs work for LDCs when member countries manufacture complementary products and are similar in terms of culture, size, access to foreign exchange, level of corruption, speed of bureaucracy, and so on. When nations are dissimilar, such as Brazil, Uruguay and Argentina, there is a short circuit between them, and the regional agreements simply do not work for long.

DONOR POLICY THAT WILL SEIZE THE OPPORTUNITY

How, then, should the United States best view LDC regional trading blocs? Between the two extremes of "they are great and improve the previous bad situation of individual country import substitution barriers," and "they are terrible and violate all sensible economic theory," a middle position exists. These agreements can play a role as a transitional device. LDC finance ministers think of them as a way to expand trade; LDC businesses think of them as an opportunity to expand profits.

As noted, regional agreements historically seem to work for a while, but not in the long term. If economic theory and ideology could be adjusted to this reality, moving us one step closer to believing that regional arrangements are useful in certain cases, then perhaps the U.S. government might help LDC regional agreements work where they are already set up. Donor countries in general could promote them, up to a point. World Bank assistance in setting up clearing mechanisms for regional trading blocs could be limited to, say, 10 years, after which the LDCs involved would agree to phase out the bloc and become more open to world competition.

This model sounds relatively simple, but it would be attacked as not being supportable by economic theory. Regardless, the proposition is consistent with current reality as LDC businesses and LDC government officials experience it.

As noted, the general attitude of the U.S. government, manifested in all policy reform negotiations with LDCs and in a variety of trade negotiations, has been that regional trading blocs are bad—that countries harm themselves and are morally culpable if they form blocs. Therefore, LDCs should not create them. This general attitude is inconsistent with the reality experienced by LDC negotiators on the other side of the table.

On hearing such reasoning from the U.S. side of the table, an LDC finance minister—whether Senegalese, Ghanaian or Bangladeshi—tends to be verbally polite. But he or she is really thinking that Americans simply do not understand the LDC reality. The underlying economic condition in the LDC is that most of its businesses cannot sell their products internationally because they do not know how to produce anything that will meet world market standards. If the LDC government uses a regional trading bloc to force its businesses to compete within a six- or eight- country boundary instead of only within its own country, these businesses will have to learn how to produce higher quality goods. Over time, they may be able to compete in the developed countries. But the LDCs are being told by the industrial nations to open up instantly and allow their businesses to compete in the global economy. The minister wonders why the developed nations do not realize that the LDC businesses will rapidly go under in these conditions.

These are the thoughts going through the minds of LDC trade experts as the U.S. explains its policies. The reactions of LDC finance ministers during formal negotiations on, for instance, breaking down Andean Pact barriers are much more polite than their reactions over dinner, which essentially are, "You people are crazy. You have no idea what it is like in the real business world in our country."

The U.S. attitude toward regional trading blocs should be considerably changed. The United States should think about them in part as a series of technical financing problems and opportunities. If one accepts the proposition that regional trading blocs—whether or not they are bad in theory—in reality come with a financial clearing mechanism, then one should realize that a new currency has been created. The question that then arises is how the amount of trade denominated in that new regional currency can be maximized, or how additionality in trade within the region can be ensured.

The U.S. government and the international institutions ought to be working hard to determine how to make such alternative currencies work to maximize trade within the region in the short run and to facilitate moves into hard currency trade in the long run. Currently, because the subject is theoretically *verboten*, no one is paying attention to the issue except the LDC businesses who actually use the informal systems.

TURNING LIABILITIES INTO ASSETS FOR U.S. BUSINESS

U.S. businesses need to realize that blocs provide new opportunities. In a bloc of, say, eight countries, one country is likely to have relatively transparent boundaries to the outside world. It is possible for a U.S. firm to invest in that country and to export to the other seven.

If a bloc exists in French West Africa, U.S. businesses have the opportunity to move into one of the member countries, export to the others, and eventually export to and invest in France, which is relatively open to these countries. The same strategy could be implemented using former British colonies in East Africa or Central Africa as bases for export to Britain. Through business relations with these trading blocs, U.S. businesses could thus develop platforms for export to the rest of Europe. Similar strategies could work in Asia, for example from Thailand or Malaysia into Japan. These LDC blocs offer an opportunity to export from them to somewhere else because at least one of the major industrial powers, whether Japan or Europe, has become relatively more open to exports from one or more countries in each bloc. But U.S. business finds it difficult to recognize these opportunities.

In addition, U.S. businesses can benefit from creative ways of sourcing by using local finance. Insofar as local currency trading exists in these countries, the possibility exists of buying products for local currency or for a clearing account transaction, on paper, that would previously have required the expenditure of hard currency. Therefore, it is possible for American businesses to design creative joint ventures with local businesses as a way to source—for free or very inexpensively or on credit terms—items they otherwise could not obtain or could obtain only for a large expenditure of hard currency. Virtually no one takes advantage of such opportunities, particularly in Latin America. However, in Latin America as well as in Africa, such strategies potentially could provide considerable returns for American businesses.

Small Latin countries, perhaps such as Ecuador, fear the extent to which the Andean Pact bureaucracy or the LAFTA bureaucracy could take over national economic policies. The African countries are upset about the extent to which the French central institutions and the French West Africa Union try to dictate their economic policies. Such fears arise because some approach to a unified regional monetary and fiscal policy is necessary to create and to manage an efficient regional economic bloc. Similar concerns preoccupy some EC members, who fear domination by the Brussels EC bureaucracy after 1992.

Perhaps there is a lesson in this for the West. If the LDC businesses are concerned, it may be because such bureaucratic central policy coordination does offer competitive opportunities for the United States. It is to the United States' advantage to be able to go to these regions and to work with an institutional bureaucracy that is relatively efficient, that tries to be economically rational and that conforms to a coherent monetary policy.

Rather than classifying the whole French bloc (as most businesses think of it) in West Africa as an impediment to the United States, U.S. business could view it as a resource that must be understood to be used: once a U.S. business understands how to get into the bloc, that business can "work" the system with the organizational assistance of competent French institutions and bureaucracy.

It is difficult to know how to urge U.S. business as a whole to rethink the conceptual framework of whether regional blocs pose a constraint or an opportunity to the United States. On an individual business level, however, the conceptual framework can be redrawn to recognize the new business opportunities that regional trading blocs can create.

In terms of national policy, the United States must rethink its attitude toward regional trading blocs in general. We should begin to see them as transition points on the way toward the global open trading system that this country desires, rather than merely as boundaries designed to exclude.

The Diversification of the Eastern European Bloc: Implications for Western Industrial Nations

11

by Rebecca S. Hartley

The Soviet economic model has become increasingly discredited even among Eastern bloc members and in the Third World. It is a compelling time to examine the regional trading bloc that comprises the countries of Eastern Europe because it is becoming clear that the West is winning the Cold War by economic rather than military strength. Formally organized as the Council for Mutual Economic Assistance, these Eastern bloc nations have historically been overwhelmingly dependent economically on trade with the Soviet Union. We will see, however, the development of a dual dependence of the CMEA countries on the West and on bilateral agreements with their own regional trading bloc partners. The political and economic changes under way within these centrally planned economies raise numerous questions in the international trade field for Western nations.

A DISSOLVING BLOC

It would be misleading to describe the CMEA as a common market because it does not maintain a common external tariff and its members are not decentralized market economies but, since World War II, have been CPEs. Nevertheless, the CMEA was established to encourage integration and specialization among the Eastern European countries, and a high percentage of member trading has been intrabloc trade. Therefore, it is reasonable to think of the CMEA as a regional trading bloc. In fact, the Western industrial nations have traditionally viewed CMEA countries as belonging to a trading (and military) bloc distinct from the rest of the world.

Certain traditional economic conventions and arrangements within the CMEA encourage the view that member countries are part of a regional bloc. These mechanisms include the USSR's transshipment of energy and raw materials as well as substantial Soviet credits to other member nations and the transferable ruble system of accounting. The TR is an artificial currency that, in fact, serves merely as an intra-CMEA accounting tool.

However, in the face of increasingly strong economic imperatives, the traditional reasons for CMEA cohesiveness are dissolving. The USSR economy grew at an annual rate of only about 1.5 percent in 1988, according to U.S. Central Intelligence Agency and Defense Intelligence Agency estimates. Indeed, with the exception of 1986, the Soviet economy has grown less than 2.5 percent annually since 1976.[1] Soviet President Gorbachev, through his announced military reductions and economic liberalization, has admitted that the Soviet communist system is in need of massive restructuring. In an effort to reform the economy, he has announced cuts in state investment, a reduction in defense expenditures and an emphasis on consumer consumption. Recently, however, he has reduced his efforts to reform prices, an indication that he is having to modify *perestroika*, or restructuring, to lessen domestic public disapproval of his overall economic proposals.

Increasingly, therefore, CMEA member countries will draw away from each other to the extent that overt Soviet power and influence in the area decrease and members require goods and hard currency that only trade with the West can provide. Yet, at the same time, new reasons will cause the members to continue their association in bilateral, albeit looser, forms. Trade with other CMEA members will prove to be an important bridging mechanism to cushion the change to convertibility of member country currencies and the transition of their economies toward market-based systems.

HISTORY OF THE CMEA

The Council for Mutual Economic Assistance was formed at Stalin's initiative in 1949. It was to be a regional group dedicated to integrating the economies of Eastern Europe and to encouraging those nations to specialize in particular areas of production. In essence, though, it was Stalin's political response to the economic assistance plan that Secretary Marshall had proposed for Europe in June 1947; in addition, it helped to solidify Soviet control over the economies of Eastern Europe. It is interesting to note that, in both Western neoclassical economic theories and Eastern bloc communism, increased specialization via international trade is a major goal.

A Soviet-oriented pact was not entirely unattractive to many Eastern European countries in 1949. The Marshall Plan had not yet produced proven advantages, and the USSR could point to its considerable growth rates during the 1930s and military successes during World War II as signs of the vitality of its economic system.

The CMEA had six charter members: the USSR, Hungary, Czechoslovakia, Romania, Bulgaria, and Poland. Five other nations later joined: Albania (1949-61), East Germany (1950), Mongolia (1962), Cuba (1972), and Vietnam (1979). Yugoslavia was granted "limited participant" status in 1965, and observer status has been granted to Angola, Ethiopia, Laos, North Korea, South Yemen, Afghanistan, and Mozambique.

In 1949, both Poland and Czechoslovakia expressed interest in joining the talks that would determine the shape of the Marshall Plan. However, under pressure from the Soviet Union, they declined to participate.[2] The remaining western and northern European countries went on to establish the interim Committee on European Economic Cooperation, which created the guiding principles for the Marshall Plan, while the eastern countries became members of the CMEA.

In practice, the CMEA did not rival the achievements of the Marshall Plan. From the time of its founding until March 1954, the CMEA's major activities were only to register the numerous bilateral commercial accords reached between the USSR and Eastern bloc countries and to solidify the region's opposition to Tito. This situation changed somewhat under Khrushchev, who recognized the importance of concrete economic and political ties between the Soviets and the satellite nations. He realized that it was to the Soviet Union's advantage not to have to shore up the Eastern bloc economies. At the March 1954 CMEA meeting, he recommended that CMEA mechanisms coordinate all national economic plans within the bloc.

Nevertheless, the goal of economic integration has never been achieved. Equally elusive has been the goal of commodity specialization. The Eastern bloc nations have often viewed investment in heavy industry as an important prerequisite to national autonomy and industrial development. In fact, even though most Eastern European countries are poorly endowed with raw materials, investment in heavy industries requiring large raw material and energy bases has historically dominated CMEA nations' domestic investment, except in Hungary and possibly Poland.[3] In addition, each nation has resisted being "tracked" in a specific direction by outsiders, even though the outsiders were communists.

The tendency of these countries to avoid specialization in areas such as agriculture or low technology manufactures in which they might have comparative advantages could perhaps be reversed through closer ties with the West. Market forces might achieve what political suggestions have not. Increased trade with the more competitive Western economies might force CMEA members to specialize in order to compete with Western goods.

EFFORTS TO INCREASE TRADE WITH THE WEST

Traditionally, CMEA's efforts have been directed toward increasing trade between member countries, while limiting hard currency trade with the West. Such policies have constrained hard currency debt and permitted the sale to other CPEs of goods that would be substandard in Western markets. The result has been a lack of industrial modernization within the CMEA nations.

Currently, between one-half of total CMEA trade and four-fifths of intrabloc trade is with the Soviet Union. However, trade with the West has been expanding for most CMEA states. In 1988, the CPEs' shares of trade with market economies as a percent of their total foreign trade ranged from 17 percent for Bulgaria and Czechoslovakia to 37 percent for Poland and Hungary.[4] These levels of trade with the West have grown because high grade materials, top quality equipment and technical expertise to operate the equipment have generally been unavailable from the USSR or other CMEA members. This trade required increasing amounts of hard currency, usually obtainable only through export sales to the West. The drive for more exports in turn increased the demand for Western technology so that the CMEA industry could produce more high quality goods. A cycle had thus been established even before the remarkable political changes in Eastern Europe in 1989.

In view of this cycle, it should not be surprising that the industrialized CMEA countries (other than East Germany and the USSR) have already established formal and informal contacts with the West through the General Agreement on Tariffs and Trade, the International Monetary Fund (IMF) and the World Bank. The USSR has considered formal GATT membership in the past, but its 1986 application to participate in the Uruguay Round was rejected. Although the United States and the EC have recently agreed to support observer status for the USSR, they have not agreed to support full membership privileges for that nation. The USSR must also obtain the support of additional GATT members as the GATT council acts by consensus. East Germany has close trade ties with the Federal Republic of Germany and will soon have economic privileges not available to other Eastern European countries because of the progress toward formal German unification.

Price Reforms

If Stalin's original intention was to provide a political framework for Eastern European cooperation that would rival Western European efforts, the present CMEA can be viewed as a failure.

However, the CMEA may provide a mechanism through which reforms can be made so that its members will eventually be free participants in the world market economy—an outcome that would shock its founder. It would be ironic if the CMEA again became simply a formal registry of bilateral trading agreements between Eastern European countries and not a mechanism to increase Soviet economic influence in the area.

To some extent, CMEA nations have been dependent on the Western market system for years. They have been unable to devise a workable intrabloc trading system using a traditional centrally planned economy method of setting prices. Instead, goods prices for their intrabloc trade are set by means of a complicated formula agreed upon in 1975, which essentially averages world market prices for the previous five years.[5] This system tends to cushion sudden shocks by inducing a price lag.

As CMEA countries try to move toward market-controlled prices, economic problems resulting from former policies are inevitable. In addition, because of extremely high levels of government subsidization of basic consumer goods and housing and inadequate levels of production of consumer products, the Eastern bloc countries cannot conduct price reform without experiencing economic crises such as hyperinflation or severe shortages.

CPEs have dealt with excess consumer demand through shortages and rationing rather than through inflation per se. But consumers have responded to the lack of goods by saving excess currency. If prices—having been held down for many years—are reformed to create a system in which the market can send appropriate signals to producers, then inflation is inevitable. Inflation invites criticism of the government and popular unrest, as has already occurred in Poland. CMEA leaders thus face the problem of how to make the transition from nonmarket to market economies and remain in power. For the foreseeable future, cautious reformers in these nations may find some of their countries' current bilateral trade agreements with other CPEs attractive in helping ensure a market for their goods that are not marketable in the West. At the same time, they may try to ship as many exports for hard currency as possible.

It is this dynamic that is behind the USSR's enthusiasm for conducting CMEA trade in hard currency after 1990. In the short term, such a change will benefit the Soviet Union because its major exports to other CMEA nations are not manufactured goods, but oil and natural gas. Thus, any price reforms in the CMEA that require traded items to be paid for in hard currency will be much more attractive to the USSR than to those countries whose main export items are manufactured goods that are sub-world standard.

Moves toward Monetary Convertibility

The Soviet Union has announced moves toward its goal of a fully convertible ruble. Gorbachev recognizes that the absence of a convertible currency hurts the willingness of Western businesses to undertake joint ventures in the USSR.[6] But moves toward convertibility will progress slowly because, although they will tend to lead toward economic independence for individual Eastern bloc countries, they will nevertheless be painful.

At the October 1987 session of the CMEA, the head of the Soviet delegation, N.I. Ryzhkov, called for the council to adopt a long-range goal of:

> gradual changeover, as the necessary conditions emerge, from the mutual convertibility of national currencies into the creation of a collective monetary unit that in the future will be convertible *(obratimy)* into freely convertible *(konvertiruyemy)* currencies. But this will take time, of course, and it will be necessary to carry out significant changes in the economic mechanisms and principles of the countries' economic interaction. . . .[7]

In light of the Soviet impetus for monetary convertibility, those regimes that wished to take steps to reform their economies had a clear signal that they could do so with reduced fear of Soviet military intervention.

CMEA members currently conduct their interbloc accounts through transferable rubles, and trade balances are rationalized at set periods. However, full convertibility is not a viable option in the near future for these communist economies—with the possible exception of East Germany, which will probably adopt the West German mark as its currency. The others will probably take intermediate steps such as setting up special economic zones or currency auctions to cushion the shock of moving from official exchange rates to black market exchange rates. As Ryzhkov states, such moves will necessitate significant changes in each country's method of economic interaction.

PRESSURES FOR CHANGE

The basic Soviet goal since World War II has been to achieve military and economic security. In the past, economic security was obtained through control of the satellites and a virtual monopoly of their trade. However, given its current economic climate, the USSR cannot afford to subsidize the faltering economies of Eastern Europe if such subsidies mean that important domestic reforms will suffer. The USSR is feeling the pains of an overextended empire.

Pressures for economic and/or political change differ greatly among CMEA member states, as do their use of market mechanisms and their degree of political openness. The Soviet Union is experiencing pressures from many areas—military, budget deficit, consumers, feuding national factions, and depressed petroleum prices. Poland, too, despite Solidarity leadership, is rapidly approaching economic catastrophe. The severity of the winter of 1989-90 may be key to the survival of the Polish, and perhaps even the Soviet, leadership. The other Eastern European states are confronting similar, though less immediately severe, economic pressures. If the CMEA countries actually make progress in increasing their use of market systems, it will not be a uniform movement. Rather, progress will be determined by the specific economic and political imperatives facing each country's leaders.

The USSR's Hard Currency Difficulties

Gorbachev's domestic economic reforms and stated objectives have reduced the overt Soviet military threat to reformers in Eastern Europe. However, Gorbachev faces pressures to raise hard currency, and this could create difficulties for the Soviet Union as well as for its allies. Over 90 percent of Soviet hard currency exports are raw materials and armaments. Falling oil prices have already hurt Soviet net investment in energy resource production by reducing the hard currency earnings from this sector. These declining earnings have in turn reduced investment in sectors that cannot immediately yield hard currency earnings.[8]

To finance *perestroika*, Gorbachev must continue to sell oil and natural gas, gold, and weapons. He will also have to borrow from the West. In addition, as discussed above, Gorbachev may find it tempting to import as many manufactured goods as possible from other CMEA countries to save hard currency and, at the same time, to switch as many USSR export goods as possible onto a hard currency price scale. Seen in this light, the recent Soviet plans for change in the CMEA are understandable. In 1988, the USSR exported more than 75 million tons of crude oil to CMEA nations.[9] If these energy exports had been purchased for hard currency at world prices, the USSR's hard currency reserves would have greatly increased.

The sale of gold may at first appear to be a solution to the USSR's hard currency difficulties. Between 1982 and 1986, Soviet gold sales tripled, from approximately 100 tons per year to approximately 300 tons per year.[10] But the sale of gold is not a practical solution for the USSR because, if continued, it would lead to a saturated world gold market that would cause declining returns from gold sales similar to those the Soviets are experiencing in energy markets. Furthermore, South Africa, the world's leading gold producer, is selling gold to replace capital that is being lost because of Western sanctions and corporate pull-outs, which place further downward pressure on the price of gold.

The Eastern European Debt Imperative

In addition to current account issues, most Eastern bloc nations face problems caused by too much foreign hard currency debt. Because of this and other factors discussed below, intra-CMEA trade will have to remain at reasonably high levels for the foreseeable future. If CPEs can obtain at least adequate goods without expending hard currency, they will be tempted to do so. Even countries such as Poland and Hungary—which desperately desire increases in their exports to the West—will feel conflicting pressures to maintain their CMEA trading relationships as a crutch. This is borne out by Hungary's negative reaction to Soviet attempts to conduct intrabloc sales of oil and natural gas in hard currency. Hungary would have a difficult time selling many of the goods it trades with other CMEA nations (especially the USSR) for hard currency. The very real problem confronting these nations is the necessity of modernizing some key industries and at the same time preventing the collapse of their economies due to deterioration in other industries or unsustainable debt.

It is useful to look at the rate of increase of foreign debt that CMEA member countries have experienced over the past few years.[11] This and similar imperatives have made the leaders of the Eastern bloc recognize that they must increase export competitiveness to service their debts and modernize their industrial infrastructure.

Bulgaria. Since 1984, Bulgaria's net foreign debt in convertible currency has more than tripled, rising to $6.2 billion at the end of 1987. The Bulgarian hard currency debt situation is likely to worsen if its intra-CMEA trade decreases. At the end of 1987, it had achieved a small surplus in merchandise trade with other CMEA members.

Bulgaria was a traditional Stalinist state until very recently. But even under First Secretary Todor Zhivkov during the period 1954-89, Bulgaria made limited efforts to attract foreign partners for joint ventures. The government has announced that, although it will keep to a CPE model, it will allow some self-administered and self-funded companies to experiment with reforms such as performance related wages. However, to date, these efforts have not been very successful, at least partly because the central authorities still issue production targets for all corporations. Bulgaria's new government has not yet presented a plan for workable reforms.

Czechoslovakia. This CMEA country has managed to maintain a relatively low level of hard currency indebtedness—approximately $4 billion at the end of 1986. Czechoslovakia is in a good position to service this debt because of the better quality of its manufactured goods compared with the other Eastern bloc countries and its relatively healthy export performance with the West. Thus, its aggressively reformist stance prior to the January 1990 CMEA negotiations is understandable. If Czechoslovakia can negotiate some form of compensation from the USSR in return for making a relatively fast switch to hard currency-denominated trade, it will be ahead of most other CMEA nations in its ability to compete in world markets. Still, it is in great need of infrastructure and industrial modernization, and this will probably necessitate importing components from the West because its manufactured goods in many vital sectors do not meet Western standards.

Until the achievement of a CMEA agreement on hard currency-denominated trade, Czechoslovakia will likely try to increase its raw material imports from other CMEA nations to effect de facto import substitution from the other CPEs. Because of its ability to export moderately for payment in hard currencies, hold hard currency indebtedness to a manageable level and export manufactured goods not salable in the West to other CMEA countries, Czechoslovakia will not be under extreme economic pressure for internal market-type reforms. This may buy the new leadership time for gradual reform measures. Eventually, however, if Czechoslovakia wishes to compete in Western markets—or even in Eastern ones—it will be forced to update its infrastructure, equipment and technology. The outcome of the spring 1990 Prague meeting of the CMEA commission will be a major factor in determining the pace of this change.

The German Democratic Republic. The GDR's gross indebtedness to the West (excluding West Germany) was approximately $15.5 billion in 1987. Its economy in 1988 grew at an annual rate of less than 1 percent after adjusting for inflation. State subsidies absorbed more than one-fifth of the national income—about 50-60 billion East German marks.[12] Little has been spent in recent years to upgrade GDR industrial production facilities and, as a result, industry infrastructure badly needs repair or replacement.

Any relative strength of the GDR economy can partially be explained by its supportive, close relationship with West Germany, and thus with the European Community. Historically, the special relationship with West Germany has provided a close example for the GDR of what a motivated workforce and a vibrant economy can produce under a market system. This example, coupled with the enormous support West Germany has offered—contingent on political and economic reforms and free elections—makes moves toward unity look quite attractive to many East Germans. Reforms gain even more appeal when considering the present protesting (and emigrating) populace, the unrealistic price system, the stagnating business climate, and the disintegrating infrastructure. The results of the March 18, 1990 elections in the GDR will determine the speed of formal steps toward German unification. Informal steps toward German unification will continue regardless of governmental changes.

Hungary. This Eastern bloc country currently owes more than $22 billion to Western creditors.[13] In the short run, it must borrow enough hard currency to service the interest payments on its debt. In the long run, it should finance the modernization of its industrial capacity. In both time frames, steps should be taken to create a climate that will encourage lenders and investors to have confidence in the economy and the government's stability. Thus, Hungary's (formerly Communist Party) leaders acknowledged in 1989 what others saw much earlier—that future economic growth in Hungary will have to be export-fueled to provide foreign exchange to avoid continued borrowing from abroad.[14]

It is true that during the mid-1980s, Hungary began significantly to improve its balance of payments denominated in hard currency. This occurred not because its export drive was successful, but rather because industrial investment was reduced and import restrictions were imposed. In addition, the forint appreciated in value throughout this period, making Hungarian exports even less competitive internationally. Tourism increased to an annual level of about $370 million.

Arguably, Hungary led the extensive political and economic reform steps among the CMEA members. The country is attempting to add incentives to encourage quality performance, especially in export industries. The parliament has voted to hold free elections in March 1990. If this occurs as planned, Hungary will, with East Germany, have the freest and most open polling in the Eastern bloc in more than 40 years.

Imre Pozsgay, a leading reformer and a member of the Politburo, has announced that the Hungarian Socialist Party (HSP)—which superseded the Hungarian Socialist Workers Party (Communist Party) in October 1989—will go into opposition if it is defeated in the parliamentary elections.[15] (It should be noted that the HSP is not guaranteed seats in the legislature, as the Polish Communist Party was in the summer 1989 Polish elections.)

According to Mr. Pozsgay, Hungary should learn from the example of Poland in the early 1980s: "Through dictatorship, power can be protected but a country cannot be made to function."[16] Thus, the major question is—can a government that is not popularly elected and that lacks the confidence of the people conduct significant reforms while undergoing the transition from a communist monopoly on political and economic power?

To some extent, this is a "chicken and egg" question. Only a government that has the people's confidence is able to ask for the major sacrifices that necessarily accompany an abrupt switch to a market economy. But that confidence may not be forthcoming until the people have some assurance that the reforms will be undertaken. Furthermore, they may be unwilling to pay the immediate price of those reforms in return for the future, and uncertain, benefits created by such changes. If results are not readily apparent and the government lacks the confidence of the people, pressure may increase for even more rapid change. A free market system cannot be imposed by central government fiat. Such a system is a political and economic evolution away from traditional CPE systems and may be achievable only through a revolution. It remains to be seen if the more traditional communists in Eastern Europe agree with Mr. Pozsgay and have the courage to act on their convictions.

Poland. This CMEA country's economy continues to suffer as a result of the major depression it experienced in the early 1980s. At the end of 1987, its hard currency debt was about $37.5 billion. Its real level of national income has still not surpassed the level achieved in 1978.

Solidarity will have a difficult time reforming the economy unless it receives substantial Western economic assistance. Poland must modernize its industrial infrastructure to compete in world markets. But to receive the necessary aid and loans from abroad, it will have to create a government with a plan that inspires confidence from both the Polish people and Western lenders. In addition, Poland will need extensive debt relief to get back on the road to development. To placate the population, the government has instituted measures such as monthly cost-of-living allowances, but these serve mainly to increase the government's deficit and to decrease the effectiveness of policies designed to reform the economy.

The success of the Solidarity-led government remains to be seen. Solidarity's essentially negative campaign—conducting the election as a referendum on the Communist Party—served to get

Solidarity deputies elected, but now they must work together to formulate a plan to reorganize the economy. Such a plan will probably cause labor distortions if it is to reduce production inefficiency. Thus, we may increasingly see conflicts between the objectives of Solidarity the "union" and Solidarity the "party."

Romania. Official government figures are difficult to verify and in some cases even more difficult to believe. For example, while Ceaucescu's government had stated a goal of significantly modernizing Romania's industrial facilities, it had also set a target of producing 90 percent of its own capital goods, creating a conflict between modernization and hard currency debt avoidance.

Under Ceaucescu, Romania undertook a largely successful program to repay its hard currency debt. It also passed a law banning foreign borrowing, implemented principally to reduce Western nations' potential leverage on Romanian human rights policies. Yet, there were contradictions in Romania's external economic relations: while undertaking a crippling debt repayment schedule, the country reversed its recent decision to reject its most-favored-nation status with the United States.

Ironically, Ceaucescu's harsh repayment plan may result in future benefits for debt-free Romania as it requests foreign assistance. But substantial progress in rebuilding cannot take place until free and fair elections produce a government that has the confidence of its people.

CHALLENGES FOR THE EASTERN BLOC

CMEA and bilateral trade arrangements can provide shelters for member country industries that produce goods which are not salable in the West. The danger for reforms and export promotion schemes is that pressure from some CMEA members (particularly the USSR) will lead those countries to export relatively high quality goods to other centrally planned economies for payment in transferable rubles at the expense of hard currency sales. The Soviet Union, an energy exporter currently with no burdensome hard currency debt, will probably push for more intra-CMEA trade in energy resources denominated in hard currencies.

On the other hand, countries with relatively large levels of debt will probably push for reforms that will allow them to increase their hard currency exports quickly and dramatically while receiving some sort of compensation for more expensive energy imports. Each of those nations will press for its competitive goods and raw material exports to be denominated in hard currency and for its substandard exports to be denominated in transferable rubles. During the transition period in which these economies are upgrading their industrial infrastructure, it will be useful for them to send goods they cannot sell elsewhere to the Soviet Union and other CMEA countries.

Thus, even the most radical reformers will need to continue close trade ties with other CMEA members. If the Eastern bloc leaders move too quickly on price reform and cause large decreases in job security, a "conservative" backlash from displaced workers in CPEs might result, especially in Poland. It is interesting to consider whether CPE workers would be as patient as Mexican workers have been recently as Mexico's standard of living plunged. According to World Bank figures, Hungary's per capita GNP was US$2,100 in 1984 and $2,240 in 1987. In contrast, Mexico's per capita GNP was US$2,200 in 1984 but had declined to $1,830 by 1987.[17]

If Eastern bloc countries begin to experience real, marked declines in per capita GNP, coupled with steep actual or disguised inflation, even those governments that have made substantial political reforms will come under extreme pressure to produce immediate results from economic reforms (exacerbated perhaps by the severity of the winter of 1989-90). During Gorbachev's May 1989 visit to China, he was viewed in that country as a guiding light for reform because of his stance in favor of political restructuring. On the other hand, he is often criticized in the USSR for moving slowly on economic reform, an area in which China had been seen as a leader. Solidarity will probably experience such political dilemmas as it tries to create effective government policies to deal with the difficult problem of economic reform.

A related danger arises from labor market distortions. Changes in current distributions of labor will occur as artificial employment is reduced. The need for increased efficiency will probably necessitate labor cuts, and this may tend to reduce wages as well as increase unemployment. Theoretically, products should become less costly and therefore more competitive in export markets. In practical terms, however, current Eastern European leaders must be concerned about the extent to which labor market changes increase popular demand for possibly reactionary political changes and undercut their power bases.

Even if Eastern European leaders recognize the importance of economic reforms, they will encounter difficulties in making them without free market mechanisms in place. As noted, the CMEA has made de facto use of Western markets to set prices. But will the Eastern bloc leadership be able to encourage the establishment of relatively free markets through evolutionary political reform? The recent chaos and bloodshed in China resulted largely from a liberalized economic program that in turn encouraged a movement for political liberalization which was unacceptable to the ruling faction. That government still had the overwhelming military power needed to suppress the reform movement. The countries in Eastern Europe no longer have this option because of the extent of political reform and because the USSR, under Gorbachev, has abandoned the Brezhnev Doctrine.

Economic change and political change in CPEs appear inseparable. As dual economies develop in Eastern European countries, the political survival of their governing parties will depend on how the leaders manage the liberalization of the private and public sectors.

CHALLENGES FOR THE WEST

It is important for the West to develop a coherent economic policy toward the CMEA countries that reflects the major thaws that have occurred in the Cold War. In this context, it is useful to consider the Eastern bloc economically as a group of developing countries—they need everything and can afford little, which gives rise to their enormous problems in setting economic priorities.

Currently, only about 1 percent of total U.S. foreign trade is with CPEs.[18] The total U.S.-USSR trade level averages between $1.9-$2.6 billion annually, of which about 50 percent is U.S. grain sales to the USSR. The United States is a partner with the Soviet Union in about 3 percent of Soviet trade with the industrialized world, whereas Western Europe shares about 90 percent of that trade. However, in light of the World Bank projection that the "industrial communist world" will include 450 million consumers by 2021, this potential market will be highly attractive to Western countries and businesses.[19]

The prospect of profits from selling goods and services to CMEA countries and the perceived reductions of the Soviet military threat have already led to a flurry of Western business investment interest in Eastern Europe. If good business climates are created, Western investment and joint ventures will help strengthen the reforming Eastern European economies.

During the height of the Cold War, it was prudent policy for the West to restrict trade to limit the transfer of sensitive technology. While it is still vital that strategic technology be kept from potentially hostile nations, it would be shortsighted for Western policymakers to deny that trade will increase with them. In addition, those nations must import currently restricted technology if they are to modernize their industries. Shortsightedness and slow-moving adaptation in COCOM, particularly if the United States stands alone, will also tend to exacerbate tensions in the West.

The United States has begun to ease restrictions on trade with the Eastern European nations (but not the USSR) along the lines of its trade guidelines for China. Regardless of changes in COCOM rules, tension between the United States and EC nations over high technology trade with Eastern Europe is likely to persist as long as COCOM restrictions exist.

Leading by Example

The West should encourage the transition of Eastern European countries to market economies, but in ways that do not compromise the inherent soundness of its own economic systems. The West has long recognized that there are only limited methods by which it can encourage or discourage political change in communist countries. The first step for the West should be to continue to lead by example—by demonstrating the advantages of market economies.

Barring major changes in current liberalizing trends, we should continue to provide humanitarian aid such as emergency food grants to Poland. We should adapt our export-import laws once we see concrete proof of changes in, for example, Eastern bloc emigration policies. We should allow Western businesses to function in a fair, open market system in relations with the Eastern bloc. In ensuring that assistance measures—such as FY 1990 and 1991 U.S. aid to Eastern Europe—remain economically sound for Western nations, we must include provisions for emergency measures to help proven reformers maintain control in the event of a threatened collapse of their economic systems.

Among the consequences of the economic collapse of any of the Eastern bloc countries are the effects on Western economies. This contingency has obviously been a factor behind the French proposal for a European development bank. The Western countries will have to keep a close watch on how aid and loan money is spent in the East. In the interest of sound policy, the West cannot afford to do more than to help the Eastern nations help themselves. We should not endeavor to shore up, through preferential loans or trade agreements, reformers who have not been popularly elected until they provide good-faith examples of their political and economic reforms. But once free and fair elections have been held, we can gradually integrate those countries into international organizations such as the IMF, the World Bank and the GATT.

Some commentators caution the West against taking actions that would strengthen the Eastern bloc economies because this might better enable those communist countries eventually to challenge the West militarily. Others worry about the economic consequences for the West if the Eastern bloc begins to produce labor-intensive goods such as textiles for export. But economic and political reforms are linked; at some point, true reforms in one area will effect reforms in the other. In any case, it is plausible that if Eastern European nations become stable, market-oriented economies, they will have an important stake in the global trading and financial systems and be more likely to share the West's economic principles.

In light of the current Uruguay Round and the European Community's 1992 program, how market-dominated systems should manage increased trade with CPEs or CPEs undergoing market-type reforms is an interesting question. Can such nations be grafted either onto the GATT system or onto Western regional trading blocs before they possess functioning market economies?

Although the GATT was based on a model of enlightened capitalism, a growing number of nations interested in the GATT have economic systems based on quite different models. We need to modify further the GATT system to make it workable for a variety of economic models, including CPEs in transition. At the same time, the GATT must not move precipitously to accept CPEs as members if they do not support a relatively free multilateral system. The West should look closely at Czechoslovakia, Romania, Hungary, and Poland, the CMEA countries that are already GATT members. An examination of their relationship with the GATT will provide valuable guidelines for constructing policies for other CMEA nations that wish to become GATT members.

An extended observer status may be a viable interim step toward full GATT membership for CPEs such as the USSR that are presently deemed not ready to share fully in the peaceful responsibilities of the multilateral trading system. However, such status does not remove the larger policy question for the West of whether USSR participation in the world economy is best regulated through bilateral or multilateral institutions. The evolution of the Eastern European regional trading bloc may help show the way to a GATT system that would accommodate Eastern European and Soviet needs and those of the present GATT signatories.

POLICYMAKING IN A PERIOD OF TRANSITION

Will liberalization—economic and political—continue? Yes, but progress will be halting. There are a number of major unknowns for policymakers in the West and the East in light of the changing political and economic conditions in Eastern Europe. Can current Eastern bloc leaders manage political reforms and openness so as to make tangible progress on the economic front?

What are the implications for Western nations of economic collapse in the East? Do economic reforms necessarily imply political reforms and, if so, to what extent? How much longer will the citizens of CMEA nations (especially the GDR) tolerate their declining standards of living? What form would any reactionary backlash take? What role(s) should these countries play in the international trading system? What role should be assigned to COCOM? To what extent are the economic and political reforms that have been made thus far in the CMEA countries reversible? Will different approaches to Eastern European changes result in a deep cleavage between the United States and the EC nations?

The West has taken fairly effective steps in response to the actual changes that have taken place in the Eastern bloc. The May 30, 1989 NATO declaration supported "offering the East Europeans student exchanges, help in joining Western economic organizations, and training programs and exchanges that will improve Eastern Europeans' understanding of Western technology, legal and political systems and business management."[20] The United States and the European Community have provided short-term surplus food aid to Poland on the condition that proceeds from its sale be used to support the expansion efforts of private producers in Poland. Deals of this type could perhaps be expanded if the Solidarity-led coalition proves to be a resilient, effective government.

The United States has promised to remove current trade restrictions from the USSR once the Supreme Soviet liberalizes emigration laws. The United States has also permitted the EXIM Bank to provide somewhat increased guarantees on trade with the Soviet Union. It has proposed immediate changes in COCOM rules governing exports to Eastern Europe. The U.S. Commerce Department now must act on applications for export decontrol within five months when an exporter presents proof that the identified product or its equivalent is available from foreign suppliers. President Bush has reiterated U.S. offers of technical assistance to speed economic reforms. Hungary has been given most-favored-nation status and has been designated to receive benefits under the General System of Preferences. The EC Commission is coordinating and broadening aid programs for Hungary and Poland.

Although these steps are not part of a new overall Western policy, they can be viewed as logical extensions of current policy. Western nations in fact have not yet adequately addressed the changes in philosophy and world organization that have accompanied *perestroika*. In the present uncertainty, the only sensible course for the West is to frame policies for the long term in the context of current changes, but to keep sight of the "worst case" consequences of those policies. The speed of new reforms is much faster than at any time since the establishment of the CMEA. But this does not mean that reforms will continue at the present pace. Rather than simply to react to changes in Eastern Europe, the Western nations have been called upon to create their own policies that will be unaffected by whatever rhetoric is currently coming from the East.

The Western countries must work together to formulate a common philosophy in keeping with their long-term goal of stability. This is not to say that the West should immediately change its policies to reflect a situation that it hopes for in the long run. Rather, it should take steps that encourage Eastern European countries to move toward market-structured economies in ways that remain consistent with this long-term objective. While historical, political and economic imperatives will probably require the Federal Republic to move very quickly to stabilize its relationship with the GDR, the West will not be under similar extreme pressures for supporting the other Eastern European countries.

Formulating a common Western philosophy is difficult, however. Most Western nations agree that changes in the Eastern bloc countries should be encouraged. The more difficult issues concern what types of assistance are appropriate. Each nation in the West—as well as each political faction within a nation—perceives different potential levels of worst case damage that could result from assistance policies.

Formerly, the Western alliance was united by the presence of the "Soviet threat" in a policy of minimal assistance to the Eastern bloc, even when reforms (such as the Prague Spring) were evident. Now that the Soviet threat is perceived to be decreasing, the worst case consequences often seem manageable in view of the potential political and economic benefits of assisting Eastern bloc nations, to say nothing of the instability that would result from Eastern European economic collapse.

It is the potential benefits from action and the disadvantages from inaction that are making the formation of a unified Western approach to Eastern Europe difficult. Whereas the "benefits" of collective policy were previously also collective, they are now much more individualized. For example, the benefits of increasing trade with the Eastern bloc are largely specific to the exporting nation. It will be hard for the West to formulate an acceptable uniform policy especially while the political and economic climates in Eastern Europe are in rapid transition and the Western nations cannot agree on a dominant consideration. Thus, as long as Western policy is mainly reactive, friction will continue within and among the Western nations.

If the recent changes in the Eastern bloc were rooted only in Gorbachev's personal philosophy, extreme caution would be in order. But *perestroika* and *glasnost* are policies that reflect Gorbachev's understanding of the USSR's economic position. His reforms, as well as those in Eastern Europe, have their base in practical economic necessity and manifest trends that had already begun to emerge. Thus, there is cause for cautious optimism.

When reconsidering its economic policy toward the Eastern bloc, the West should take into account these economic realities. However, it must not dismiss the political or military realities of the past 40 years. The current changes in the Eastern bloc mean that Western policymakers now confront a situation that has many more variables and far fewer constants than in the past. The West should recognize that, to remain effective, its policy must undergo a gradual evolution rather than a metamorphosis.

If economic liberalization eventually leads to stable political liberalization, then the world will be well on the path to a real thawing of relations. But in the current period of marked daily change, the West must avoid becoming entangled in retrenchments. If we are unduly entranced with the "two steps forward" that many CMEA countries are taking, we could get caught if and when some take a step backward. For now at least, the West should concentrate on helping the nations of Eastern Europe learn to help themselves.

NOTES

1. "The Soviet Economy in 1988: Gorbachev Changes Course," a report by the Central Intelligence Agency and the Defense Intelligence Agency presented to the Subcommittee on National Security Economics of the Joint Economic Committee, April 14, 1989, p. 2.
2. Harry Bayard Price, *The Marshall Plan and Its Meaning* (Ithaca, N.Y.: Cornell University Press, 1955), p. 27.
3. Richard F. Staar, *Communist Regimes in Eastern Europe*, Fifth Edition (Stanford, Ca.: Stanford University Press, 1988), p. 295.
4. Dresdner Bank, *Annual Report 1988*, p. 26.
5. Sarah Meiklejohn Terry, ed., *Soviet Policy in Eastern Europe* (New Haven, Conn.: Yale University Press, 1984), p. 168.
6. "Rumbles in the Empire," *The Wall Street Journal*, June 15, 1989, p. A12.
7. "CMEA Acts to Revamp Bloc Cooperation," *The Current Digest of the Soviet Press* (Vol. 39, No. 41), 1987, p. 10.
8. "Exploding Exports: Soviet Oil and Gas," *The Economist*, June 17, 1989, p. 83.
9. Francis X. Clines, "Soviets and Partners Say COMCON Needs Repair," *The New York Times*, January 9, 1990, p. A13.
10. Judy Shelton, *The Coming Soviet Crash: Gorbachev's Desperate Pursuit of Credit in Western Financial Markets* (New York: Free Press, 1989), p. 87.
11. Some data from Hungary, Poland and to some extent Romania are available from the IMF, which make trends in these countries easier to trace.
12. Henry Kamm, "In Hungary, the Political Changes are Tempered by Economic Fear," *The New York Times*, May 15, 1989, p. A1.
13. John Lloyd, "Hungary Vows to Free Economy," *The Financial Times*, August 3, 1989, p. 2.

14. Kamm, "In Hungary," p. A1.
15. *The Financial Times*, June 23, 1989, p. 3.
16. John Lloyd, "Hungarian Liberal With Eyes Turned Westward," *The Financial Times*, April 27, 1989, p. 2.
17. *World Development Report*, for years 1980 through 1989 (New York: Oxford University Press for the World Bank).
18. Dresdner Bank, *Annual Report 1988*, p. 26.
19. World Bank, *World Population Projections 1984*.
20. *The New York Times*, May 31, 1989, p. A1.

Regionalism: Motivations and Risks

12

by Peter Morici

The undercurrent of regionalism prevalent today in the international trading system is motivated by the political and economic problems associated with genuine multilateral progress. It entails important risks.

TOUGH SLEDDING IN THE GATT NEGOTIATIONS

Among the primary forces behind regionalism are the increased diversity of the GATT's membership and the complexity of the issues in modern trade negotiations. The Uruguay Round, with 96 members participating, involves a much greater range of nations than early GATT rounds. These nations vary significantly in their development prospects, legal and political institutions and foreign policy objectives. In addition, the agenda for trade talks has broadened to include exceedingly complex nontariff issues. Progress in areas such as intellectual property rights, government procurement and subsidies requires nations to harmonize domestic policies, practices and regulations, and to bridge large gaps in their legal and regulatory regimes and their approaches to industrial policy.

At the same time, growth is much slower and unemployment is much greater today in most of the GATT's core markets—the Organization for Economic Cooperation and Development countries—than it was in the 1950s and 1960s. Growth in real incomes and employment opportunities is necessary to cope with the adjustment costs imposed by trade liberalization.

These trends have combined to make further multilateral liberalization economically painful, politically costly and frustratingly slow. As a result, regional arrangements—such as the European Community, the U.S.-Canada Free Trade Agreement, the Australia-New Zealand Agreement, and the informal expansion of trade and investment ties in East Asia—have become attractive to policymakers. Regional agreements are looked to because:

- they provide some of the benefits of multilateral liberalization with more predictable and controllable adjustment costs; and

- they bring together smaller groups of countries with less diversity than is present in the GATT membership. This either circumvents or makes easier the technical problems of harmonization associated with nontariff barriers.

NEW REGIONAL AGREEMENTS

What are the prospects for U.S. involvement in other regional arrangements? What are the risks to the GATT system if the number of regional agreements grows?

The FTA, the EC 1992 program and the Australia-New Zealand Agreement are attractive to political leaders because the anticipated balance of benefits and costs is perceived to be predictable and favorable. Negotiators are dealing with countries and regions that share a great deal in terms of their political cultures and legal institutions. Within these groups, it is easier to bridge the differences and establish the basis for compromise on matters such as product standards, investment and services.

These kinds of favorable conditions plainly are not present among the suggested partners for the United States in new bilateral agreements. Japan, the East Asian NIEs, ASEAN, and Mexico could all impose substantially greater adjustment costs on American business and labor than will Canada if they are afforded the same market access that Canada has under the FTA. Considering the problems of interfacing the U.S. economic and legal institutions with the institutions of any of these countries or groups of countries, there is considerable potential for an imbalance of benefits and costs. Due to its more transparent economic and legal institutions, the United States could easily become a vulnerable partner in a bilateral pact with, for example, Japan.

A U.S.-Mexico FTA?

The only viable candidate for a major new FTA with the United States is Mexico. Although lacking comparable political cultures and legal institutions, both countries have strong incentives to bridge the differences. These motivations could substitute for a common heritage in the political calculus of negotiations.

The U.S. and Mexican economies are already substantially integrated. Labor and investment flows have substituted, to a certain degree, for trade flows that have been inhibited by import barriers on both sides. However, the United States must eventually accept Mexico's goods or more immigration. Whereas the United States can avoid the consequences of low wages, political unrest and economic change in the East Asian NIEs, it simply cannot avoid them in Mexico.

The economic pressures on the Mexican government to continue structural reforms are substantial and growing. The success of these reforms, however, requires expanding access to the U.S. market. The proportion of Mexicans with vested interests in opening up trade with the United States increases as the process of liberalization unfolds.

The United States has a stake in Mexican progress that far surpasses its stake in any other developing country. This reality is enough to warrant a special stance toward Mexico. America must be responsive to Mexico's economic and political requirements.

Nevertheless, the consequences of change in Mexico should not be overestimated. It will be a long time before Mexico's political situation permits its leaders to accept the kinds of commitments an FTA requires in areas such as energy, investment and services. Still, there is room for movement. Mexican attitudes have changed, and it is important to remember that the United States and Canada did not embark on the road to free trade only several years ago. The journey began much earlier with, for example, reciprocal tariff reduction agreements in 1935 and 1938, the defense production sharing agreement in 1959, and the Automotive Agreement in 1965.

FOUR QUESTIONS

What risks do regional agreements pose? If multilateral liberalization is the ultimate goal, four questions should be asked about evolving and proposed agreements.

Does the agreement raise barriers to nonmember countries? No agreement is completely clean in this regard. However, such distortions should be kept to a minimum and should be offset by other concessions or broader gains to nonmember states. A broader gain might be dynamic growth effects. For example, the creation of the EC did impose some new impediments to trade with outside countries, but these have been more than offset by the increased market opportunities created by a more prosperous European market.

Does the agreement foster stronger economies that are better able to accept adjustment in the future and better able to participate in broader multilateral liberalization?

Does the agreement address nontariff issues in a manner consistent with progress under the GATT? For example, in making national standards more compatible, liberalizing services or addressing investment issues, are the regional rules and procedures in line with current GATT requirements as well as with the approaches under consideration in multilateral discussions?

Do concessions that member countries make to each other preclude broader liberalization under the GATT? Future progress in the GATT could upset the balance of benefits achieved within a regional agreement. More plainly, do regional agreements create disincentives for participation in the GATT negotiations?

In general, the U.S.-Canada FTA stands up well to these tests. The automotive rules notwithstanding, the FTA does not increase protection vis-a-vis third countries. Its provisions are broadly consistent with GATT disciplines, and its agenda for liberalization is complementary to the Uruguay Round in its objectives and approaches. This is reflected in the FTA's positive reception by U.S. trading partners. The FTA should significantly strengthen the competitiveness of the Canadian economy, improving its capacity to accept adjustments and to participate in broader multilateral liberalization. It also does not create disincentives or obstacles for U.S. participation in multilateral progress. Canada is only 20 percent of the U.S. foreign market, and it does not serve U.S. interests to stop at that point. Furthermore, due to the well-known Canadian concerns about dependence on the United States, the FTA does not diminish Canadian interest in the GATT.

The jury is still out on EC 1992. A more fully integrated European market will strengthen the competitiveness of the individual EC economies and provide the economic basis for more outward-looking policies in the long run. However, the additional industrial and institutional adjustment required by the sweeping scope of 1992 will add to adjustment pressures in the EC. This could constrain the EC's political and economic capacity to accept any further adjustments that might be imposed by the Uruguay Round.

In addition, the EC 1992 process has caused considerable uncertainty and concern among third countries in areas including product standards, business services and the import barriers imposed by individual EC countries regarding, for instance, automobiles. Certainly, many American companies are going to invest in Europe, establishing plants there to get inside the wall. The question that has not yet been answered is: will that always work—that is, will the U.S. be able to export over the wall?

An important advantage that Europe now has is that its newest members are NIEs—Spain, Portugal and Greece. These countries have the potential to join the dynamic Italian economy in putting positive, but not overwhelming, pressure on northern EC states. After 1992, procurement barriers will no longer shield French and West German manufacturers from products made on the Iberian peninsula. Europe will clearly have to accept more of the structural adjustment that advanced industrializing countries have heretofore been reluctant to accept. Mexico could provide the United States with that kind of dynamic impulse for change.

A U.S.-Mexico or a U.S.-Canada-Mexico agreement, if appropriately structured, could stand up well. The agreement could be fashioned to be broadly consistent with GATT disciplines and complementary in its approaches to the GATT. Such an agreement need not increase production from off-shore competition. Yet, it could strengthen the competitiveness of both the Mexican and the U.S.-Canadian economies.

In the short run, though, the real questions are: would the United States turn inward in the context of such an agreement? Would the use of U.S. grey-area actions, safeguards and other trade remedy laws become more draconian as the United States absorbed the consequences of liberalization with Mexico? Would an agreement with Mexico sap the U.S. capacity for adjustment and reduce the U.S. desire for multilateral liberalization?

THE BOTTOM LINE

This brings to the foreground the real problems associated with regional agreements. The conclusion of a third, fourth or fifth agreement could significantly reduce the preferences afforded, and the expectations engendered, by earlier agreements. Although the Canada-U.S. FTA does not give Canada proprietary rights to preferential treatment in the American market, Canada's concerns would have to be considered if the United States negotiates with Mexico. The same would be true for Mexico if that nation were brought inside a North American free trade area. Essentially, the United States would have a re-contracting problem every time it sought to negotiate another arrangement.

Moreover, if, for example, the United States, Japan and the EC were to negotiate a series of bilateral deals in areas such as product standards and investment rules, those agreements would likely differ enough to prove incompatible in a multilateral context. The eggs could become fundamentally scrambled, precluding progress under the GATT.

The bottom line is that the United States should complete the Uruguay Round as best it can. It should not accept an outcome that excludes substantial progress in vital areas such as agriculture, services and intellectual property rights. In addition, it makes sense to explore ways to open up trade with Mexico. But the United States should not look further for bilateral partners—lest it builds a succession of agreements that simply will not add up to anything workable in a multilateral framework.

Appendix I

GATT Part III, Article XXIV

Territorial Application—Frontier Traffic—Customs Unions and Free-Trade Areas

(The GATT regulations regarding regional trading blocs follow.)

1. The provisions of this Agreement shall apply to the metropolitan customs territories of the contracting parties and to any other customs territories in respect of which this Agreement has been accepted under Article XXVI or is being applied under Article XXXIII or pursuant to the Protocol of Provisional Application. Each such customs territory shall, exclusively for the purposes of the territorial application of this Agreement, be treated as though it were a contracting party; Provided that the provisions of this paragraph shall not be construed to create any rights or obligations as between two or more customs territories in respect of which this Agreement has been accepted under Article XXVI or is being applied under Article XXXIII or pursuant to the Protocol of Provisional Application by a single contracting party.

2. For the purposes of this Agreement customs territory shall be understood to mean any territory with respect to which separate tariffs or other regulations of commerce are maintained for a substantial part of the trade of such territory with other territories.

3. The provisions of this Agreement shall not be construed to prevent:

a. Advantages accorded by any contracting party to adjacent countries in order to facilitate frontier traffic;

b. Advantages accorded to the trade with the Free Territory of Trieste by countries contiguous to that territory, provided that such advantages are not in conflict with the Treaties of Peace arising out of the Second World War.

4. The contracting parties recognize the desirability of increasing freedom of trade by the development, through voluntary agreements, of closer integration between the economies of the countries party to such agreements. They also recognize that the purpose of a customs union or of a free-trade area should be to facilitate trade between the constituent territories and not to raise barriers to the trade of other contracting parties with such territories.

5. Accordingly, the provisions of this Agreement shall not prevent, as between the territories of contracting parties, the formation of a customs

union or of a free-trade area or the adoption of an interim agreement necessary for the formation of a customs union or of a free-trade area, provided that:

a. With respect to a customs union, or an interim agreement leading to the formation of a customs union, the duties and other regulations of commerce imposed at the institution of any such union or interim agreement in respect of trade with contracting parties not party to such union or agreement shall not on the whole be higher or more restrictive than the general incidence of the duties and regulations of commerce applicable in the constituent territories prior to the formation of such union or the adoption of such interim agreement, as the case may be;

b. With respect to a free-trade area, or an interim agreement leading to the formation of a free-trade area, the duties and other regulations of commerce maintained in each of the constituent territories and applicable at the formation of such a free-trade area or the adoption of such an interim agreement to the trade of contracting parties not included in such area or not party to such agreement shall not be higher or more restrictive than the corresponding duties and other regulations of commerce existing in the same constituent territories prior to the formation of the free-trade area, or interim agreement, as the case may be; and

c. Any interim agreement referred to in sub-paragraphs (a) and (b) shall include a plan and schedule for the formation of such a customs union or of such a free-trade area within a resonable length of time.

6. If, in fulfilling the requirements of sub-paragraph 5(a), a contracting party proposes to increase any rate of duty inconsistently with the provisions of Article II, the procedure set forth in Article XXVIII shall apply. In providing for compensatory adjustment, due account shall be taken of the compensation already afforded by the reductions brought about in the corresponding duties of the other constituents of the union.

7. (a) Any contracting party deciding to enter into a customs union or free-trade area, or an interim agreement leading to the formation of such a union or area, shall promptly notify the contracting parties and shall make available to them such information regarding the proposed union or area as will enable them to make such reports and recommendations to contracting parties as they may deem appropriate.

(b) If, after having studied the plan and schedule included in an interim agreement referred to in paragraph 5 in consultation with the parties to that agreement and taking due account of the information made available in accordance with the provisions of sub-paragraph (a), the contracting parties find that such agreement is not likely to result in the formation of a customs union or of a free-trade area within the period contemplated by the parties to the agreement or that such period is not a reasonable one, the contracting parties shall make recommendations to the parties to the agreement. The parties shall not maintain or put into force, as the case may be, such agreement if they are not prepared to modify it in accordance with these recommendations.

(c) Any substantial change in the plan or schedule referred to in paragraph 5(c) shall be communicated to the contracting parties, which may request the contracting parties concerned to consult with them if the change seems likely to jeopardize or delay unduly the formation of the customs union or of the free-trade area.

8. For the purposes of this Agreement:

(a) A customs union shall be understood to mean the substitution of a single customs territory for two or more customs territories, so that

(i) duties and other restrictive regulations of commerce (except, where necessary, those permitted under Articles XI, XII, XIII, XIV, XV and XX) are eliminated with respect to substantially all the trade between the constituent territories of the union or at least with respect to substantially all the trade in products originating in such territories; and,

(ii) subject to the provisions of paragraph 9, substantially the same duties and other regulations of commerce are applied by each of the members of the union to the trade of territories not included in the union;

(b) A free-trade area shall be understood to mean a group of two or more customs territories in which the duties and other restrictive regulations of commerce (except, where necessary, those permitted under Articles XI, XII, XIII, XV and XX) are eliminated on substantially all the trade between the constituent territories in products originating in such territories.

9. The preferences referred to in paragraph 2 of Article I shall not be affected by the formation of a customs union or of a free-trade area but may be eliminated or adjusted by means of negotiations with contracting parties affected. This procedure of negotiations with affected contracting parties shall, in particular, apply to the elimination of preferences required to conform with the provisions of paragraph 8(a)(i) and paragraph 8(b).

10. The contracting parties may by a two-thirds majority approve proposals which do not fully comply with the requirements of paragraphs 5 to 9 inclusive, provided that such proposals lead to the formation of a customs union or of a free-trade area in the sense of this Article.

11. Taking into account the exceptional circumstances arising out of the establishment of India and Pakistan as independent States and recognizing the fact that they have long constituted an economic unit, the contracting parties agree that the provisions of this Agreement shall not prevent the two countries from entering into special arrangements with respect to the trade between them, pending the establishment of their mutual trade relations on a definitive basis.

12. Each contracting party shall take such reasonable measures as may be available to it to ensure observance of the provisions of this Agreement by the regional and local governments and authorities within its territory.

Appendix II

Preferential Trade Agreements Notified to the GATT

Agreement	Date Signed
France-Italy	
Customs union interim agreement	September 13, 1947
Customs union agreement	March 26, 1949
South African-Southern Rhodesian Customs union (Authorized continuation until the 10th session)	December 6, 1948
Nicaragua and El Salvador	March 9, 1951
European Economic Community (EEC)	March 25, 1957
European Atomic Energy Community	March 25, 1957
Central American Free Trade Area Participation of Nicaragua and Nicaraguan import duties	June 10, 1958
European Free Trade Association (EFTA)	January 4, 1960
Latin American Free Trade Area	February 18, 1960
European Free Trade Association Association with Finland	March 27, 1961
European Economic Community Association with Greece	July 9, 1961
European Economic Community Association agreements with African and Malagasy states and overseas countries and territories	July 20, 1963 February 25, 1964
European Economic Community Association with Turkey	September 12, 1963
Arab Common Market	August 13, 1964
Central African Economic and Customs Union	December 8, 1964
New Zealand-Australia Free Trade Agreement	August 31, 1965
United Kingdom-Ireland Free Trade Area Agreement	December 14, 1965
Caribbean Free Trade Agreement	Circa 1968
European Economic Community	
Associations with Tunisia and Morocco	March 28, 1969 March 31, 1969
European Economic Community Association with African and Malagasy states	July 29, 1969
European Economic Community Association with Tanzania, Uganda and Kenya	September 24, 1969

Accession of Iceland to EFTA and Association of Finland with EFTA (FINEFTA)	December 4, 1969
European Economic Community Agreement with Israel	June 29, 1970
European Economic Community Agreement with Spain	June 29, 1970
European Economic Community Association with non-European countries and territories	September 29, 1970
European Economic Community Association with Malta	December 5, 1970
European Economic Community Association with Turkey	July 27, 1971
European Communities Agreements with Austria	July 22, 1972
European Communities Agreements with Iceland	July 22, 1972
European Communities Agreements with Portugal	July 22, 1972
European Communities Agreements with Sweden	July 22, 1972
European Communities Agreements with Switzerland and Liechtenstein	July 22, 1972
European Economic Community Agreement with Egypt	December 18, 1972
European Economic Community Agreement with Lebanon	December 18, 1972
European Economic Community Association with Cyprus	December 19, 1972
European Communities Agreements with Norway	May 14, 1973
European Communities Association with Turkey	June 30, 1973
Caribbean Community and Common Market	July 4, 1973
European Communities Agreements with Finland	October 5, 1973
Agreements between Finland and Hungary	May 2, 1974
Agreement between Finland and Czechoslovakia	September 19, 1974
Africa-Caribbean-Pacific (ACP)-EEC Convention of Lomé	February 28, 1975
Agreement between Finland and the German Democratic Republic	March 4, 1975
European Economic Community Association with Greece	April 28, 1975
European Communities Agreement with Israel	May 11, 1975
Bangkok Agreement	July 31, 1975
Australia-Papua New Guinea Trade and Commercial Relations Agreement	November 6, 1976

European Communities Agreement with Tunisia	April 25, 1976
European Communities Agreement with Algeria	April 26, 1976
European Communities Agreement with Morocco	April 27, 1976
European Economic Community Agreement with Portugal	September 20, 1976
Agreement between Finland and Poland	September 29, 1976
European Economic Community Agreement with Egypt	January 18, 1977
European Economic Community Agreement with Syria	January 18, 1977
European Economic Community Agreement with Jordan	January 18, 1977
Association of Southeast Asian Nations (ASEAN) Preferential Trading Arrangements	February 24, 1977
European Economic Community Agreement with Lebanon	May 3, 1977
Accession of Greece to the European Communities	May 28, 1979
Agreement between EFTA countries and Spain	June 26, 1979
ACP-EEC Second Convention of Lomé	October 31, 1979
European Communities Agreement with Yugoslavia	February 25, 1980
Australia-New Zealand Closer Economic Relations Trade Agreement	March 28, 1983
ACP-EEC Third Convention of Lomé	December 8, 1984
Free Trade Area Agreement between Israel and the United States	April 22, 1985
Accession of Spain and Portugal to the European Communities	June 12, 1985
Canada-United States Free Trade Agreement	January 2, 1988

Sources: Jeffrey J. Schott, ed., *Free Trade Areas and U.S. Trade Policy* (Washington, D.C.: Institute for International Economics, 1989), pp. 376-383; and GATT, Basic Instruments and selected documents, various issues.

Selected Bibliography

Arbruster, Bill. "Trade Talk." *The Washington Post.* March 30, 1989.

Aslund, Anders. *Private Enterprise in Eastern Europe.* New York: St. Martin's Press, 1985.

Baker, James. "The Geopolitical Implications of the U.S.-Canada Trade Pact." *The International Economy.* January-February 1988.

Balassa, Bela. "The Conditions for the Success of Perestroika." *Global Economic Policy.* May 1989.

Belous, Richard S. *The Contingent Economy: The Growth of the Temporary, Part-Time and Subcontracted Workforce.* Washington, D.C.: National Planning Association, 1989.

Belous, Richard S. and Wyckoff, Andrew W. "Trade Has Job Winners Too." *Across the Board.* September 1987.

Brzezinski, Zbigniew K. *The Soviet Bloc: Unity and Conflict.* Rev. Ed. Cambridge, Mass.: Harvard University Press, 1981.

Calingaert, Michael. *The 1992 Challenge from Europe: Development of the European Community's Internal Market.* Washington, D.C.: National Planning Association, 1988.

Central Intelligence Agency, Defense Intelligence Agency. "The Soviet Economy in 1988: Gorbachev Changes Course." A report submitted to the Subcommittee on National Security Economics of the Joint Economic Committee. April 14, 1989.

Chote, Pat and Linger, Juyne. "Tailored Trade: Dealing with the World as It Is." *Harvard Business Review.* January-February 1988.

"CMEA Acts to Revamp Bloc Cooperation." *The Current Digest of the Soviet Press.* 39:41 (1987).

Commission of the European Communities. *The European Community.* Brussels, 1987.

Cooper, William H. *Taiwan-U.S. Free Trade Area: Economic Effects and Related Issues.* Report No. 89-96 E. Washington, D.C.: U.S. Library of Congress, Congressional Research Service, 1989.

Destler, I.M. *American Trade Politics: System Under Stress.* Washington, D.C.: Institute for International Economics, 1986.

Destler, I.M. and Odell, John A. *Anti-Protection: Changing Forces in United States Trade Politics.* Washington, D.C.: Institute for International Economics, 1987.

Diebold, William, Jr. "The History of the Issue." In *Bilateralism, Multilateralism and Canada in U.S. Trade Policy.* Ed. William Diebold, Jr. Cambridge, Mass.: Ballinger Publishing Co., 1988.

Dresdner Bank. *Annual Report.* 1988.

Feldstein, Martin and Horioka, Charles. "Domestic Saving and International Capital Flows." *Economic Journal.* June 1985.

Freeman, Richard B. and Medoff, James L. *What Do Unions Do?* New York: Basic Books, 1984.

Geiger, Theodore. *The Future of the International System: The United States and the World Political Economy*. Boston: Unwin Hyman, 1988.

Gilpin, Robert. *The Political Economy of International Relations*. Princeton: Princeton University Press, 1987.

Helliwell, John F. "From Now Till Then: Globalization and Economic Cooperation." *Canadian Public Policy*. XV Supplement. February 1989.

Keynes, John Maynard. *The General Theory of Employment, Interest, and Money*. New York: Harcourt, Brace and World, Inc., 1965.

Kindleberger, Charles P. *International Economics*. Homewood, Ill.: Richard D. Irwin, Inc., 1968.

————. *The World Depression: 1929-1939*. Berkeley, Ca.: University of California Press, 1973.

Kochan, Thomas A., Katz, Harry C. and McKersie, Robert B. *The Transformation of American Industrial Relations*. New York: Basic Books, 1986.

Krugman, Paul R., ed. *Strategic Trade Policy and the New International Economics*. Cambridge, Mass.: MIT Press, 1986.

Krugman, Paul R. and Obstfeld, Maurice. *International Economics: Theory and Policy*. Glenview, Ill.: Scott, Foresman and Company, 1988.

Kunihiro, Michihiko. "The External Implications of the Single European Market: A View from Japan." Statement by Michihiko Kunihiro, Deputy Minister for Foreign Affairs, given at the Royal Institute of International Affairs, October 11, 1988.

Kuttner, Robert. *Managed Trade and Economic Sovereignty*. Washington, D.C.: Economic Policy Institute, 1989.

Levinson, Marc. "Is Strategic Trade Fair Trade?" *Across the Board*. June 1988.

Lea, Sperry. "A Historical Perspective." In *Perspectives on a U.S.-Canadian Free Trade Agreement*. Ed. Robert M. Stern et al. Washington, D.C. and Ottawa, Ont.: Brookings Institution and Institute for Research on Public Policy, 1987.

Lendvay-Zwickl, Judith. *How Well Do We Compete? Relative Labour Costs in Canada and the United States*. Ottawa, Ont.: Conference Board of Canada, 1988.

Lipsey, Richard G. and York, Robert C. *Evaluating the Free Trade Deal: A Guided Tour through the Canada-U.S. Agreement*, Toronto, Ont.: C.D. Howe Institute, 1988.

Lipsey, Richard G. and Dobson, Wendy, eds. *Shaping Comparative Advantage*. Toronto, Ont.: C.D. Howe Institute, 1987.

Long, Olivier. *Law and Its Limitations in the GATT Multilateral Trade System*. Dordrecht, the Netherlands: Martinus Nijhoff Publishers, 1987.

Lovenduski, Joni and Woodall, Jean. *Politics and Society in Eastern Europe*. Bloomington: Indiana University Press, 1987.

McCrea, Barbara, Plano, Jack C. and Klein, George. *The Soviet and East European Political Dictionary*. Santa Barbara, Ca.: Stanford University Press, 1988.

Nanto, Dick K. *European Community-Japan Trade Relations: A European Perspective*. Report No. 86-166 E. Washington, D.C.: U.S. Library of Congress, Congressional Research Service, 1986.

———. *Japan-South Korea Economic Relations: South Korea's Approach to the "Japan Problem."* Report No. 87-953 E. Washington, D.C.: U.S. Library of Congress, Congressional Research Service, 1987.

Office of Technology Assessment. *Technology and East-West Trade: An Update*. Washington, D.C., 1983.

Ostry, Sylvia. "Global Trends: Global Solutions." Notes of an address at Queen's University, School of Policy Studies, Inaugural Conference, 1989.

Porter, Michael E. *Competitive Strategy: Techniques for Analyzing Industries and Competitors*. New York: Free Press, 1980.

Price, Harry Bayard. *The Marshall Plan and Its Meaning*. Ithaca, N.Y.: Cornell University Press, 1955.

Reisman, Simon. "Canada-United States Free Trade." In *The Issue of Free Trade in U.S.-Canadian Relations: Next Step?* Ed. Earl Fried and Paul Triziese. Washington, D.C.: Brookings Institution, 1984.

Rockwell, Keith M. "Congress Wants Japan on Unfair Trade List." *Journal of Commerce*. May 1, 1989.

Samuelson, Paul A. and Nordhaus, William D. *Economics*. New York: McGraw-Hill Book Co., 1985.

Sanford, William F. *The Marshall Plan: Origins and Implementation*. Washington, D.C.: Government Printing Office, 1987.

Schott, Jeffrey J. "More Free Trade Areas?" In *Free Trade Areas and U.S. Trade Policy*. Ed. Jeffrey J. Schott. Washington, D.C.: Institute for International Economics, 1989.

Scott, Bruce R. "National Strategies: Key to International Competition." In *U.S. Competitiveness in the World Economy*. Ed. Bruce R. Scott and George C. Lodge. Boston: Harvard Business School Press, 1985.

Shelton, Judy. *The Coming Soviet Crash: Gorbachev's Desperate Pursuit of Credit in Western Financial Markets*. New York: Free Press, 1989.

Smith, Adam. *The Wealth of Nations*. New York: Modern Library, 1965.

Smith, Murray G. *"What Is at Stake?"* In *Bilateralism, Multilateralism and Canada in U.S. Trade Policy*. Ed. William Diebold, Jr. Cambridge, Mass.: Ballinger Publishing Co., 1988.

Staar, Richard F. *Communist Regimes in Eastern Europe*. Fifth Edition. Stanford, Ca.: Stanford University Press, 1988.

Stevenson, Adlai and Frye, Alton. "Trading With Communists." *Foreign Affairs*. Spring 1989.

Terry, Sarah Meiklejohn, ed. *Soviet Policy in Eastern Europe.* New Haven: Yale University Press, 1984.

Thurow, Lester. In *World Link.* June 1989.

Tiraspolsky, Anita. "An Evaluation of Gains and Losses in Intra-CMEA Trade: Terms of Trade from 1970 to 1982." *Soviet and East European Foreign Trade.* Winter 1984-85.

Tumlir, Jan. "International Economic Order: Can the Trend Be Reversed?" *The World Economy.* March 1982.

Tyson, Laura D'Andrea. "The Debt Crisis and Adjustment Responses in Eastern Europe." *International Organization.* Spring 1986.

U.S. International Trade Commission. *The Pros and Cons of Entering into Negotiations on Free Trade Area Agreements with Taiwan, the Republic of Korea and ASEAN, or the Pacific Rim Region in General.* USITC Pub. 2166. Washington, D.C., 1989.

———. *Pros and Cons of Initiating Negotiations with Japan to Explore the Possibility of a U.S.-Japan Free Trade Area Agreement.* USITC Pub. 2120. Washington, D.C., 1988.

Viner, Jacob. *The Customs Union Issue.* New York: Carnegie Endowment for International Peace, 1953.

World Bank. *World Population Projections.* 1984.

Young, Hugo. *One of Us: A Biography of Margaret Thatcher.* London: MacMillan, 1989.

National Planning Association

NPA is an independent, private, nonprofit, nonpolitical organization that carries on research and policy formulation in the public interest. NPA was founded during the Great Depression of the 1930s when conflicts among the major economic groups—business, labor, agriculture—threatened to paralyze national decisionmaking on the critical issues confronting American society. It was dedicated to the task of getting these diverse groups to work together to narrow areas of controversy and broaden areas of agreement as well as to map out specific programs for action in the best traditions of a functioning democracy. Such democratic and decentralized planning, NPA believes, involves the development of effective governmental and private policies and programs not only by official agencies but also through the independent initiative and cooperation of the main private sector groups concerned. To preserve and strengthen American political and economic democracy, the necessary government actions have to be consistent with, and stimulate the support of, a dynamic private sector.

NPA brings together influential and knowledgeable leaders from business, labor, agriculture, and the applied and academic professions to serve on policy committees. These committees identify emerging problems confronting the nation at home and abroad and seek to develop and agree upon policies and programs for coping with them. The research and writing for these committees are provided by NPA's professional staff and, as required, by outside experts.

In addition, NPA's professional staff undertakes research designed to provide data and ideas for policymakers and planners in government and the private sector. These activities include research on national goals and priorities, productivity and economic growth, welfare and dependency problems, employment and manpower needs, and technological change; analyses and forecasts of changing international realities and their implications for U.S. policies; and analyses of important new economic, social and political realities confronting American society. In developing its staff capabilities, NPA has increasingly emphasized two related qualifications. First is the interdisciplinary knowledge required to understand the complex nature of many real-life problems. Second is the ability to bridge the gap between theoretical or highly technical research and the practical needs of policymakers and planners in government and the private sector.

All NPA reports are authorized for publication in accordance with procedures laid down by the Board of Trustees. Such action does not imply agreement by NPA board or committee members with all that is contained therein unless such endorsement is specifically stated.

NPA Board of Trustees and Officers